ASSESSMENT AND LEARNING

The assessment of what children have learned has become an important issue in education in the last few years, and this book addresses both formal and informal ways of assessing children's work and progress.

The book is divided into six units which address topics such as: principles and purposes of assessment; written, oral and practical evaluation; self-assessment; the 'whole school' approach; and staff development and appraisal.

The inclusion of practical activities, discussion topics, photographs, cartoons and case examples makes this a very user-friendly book for both trainee and experienced teachers in primary and secondary schools.

Ted Wragg is Professor of Education at Exeter University.

All teachers need to master certain basic pedagogical skills. This set of innovative yet practical resource books for teachers covers each of those skills in turn. Each book contains

- Practical, written and oral activities for individual and group use at all stages of professional development
- Transcripts of classroom conversation and teacher feedback and photographs of classroom practice to stimulate discussion
- Succinct and practical explanatory text

Other titles in the series

TALKING AND LEARNING IN GROUPS	*Elisabeth Dunne and Neville Bennett*
CLASS MANAGEMENT	*E.C. Wragg*
EXPLAINING	*E.C. Wragg and George Brown*
QUESTIONING	*George Brown and E.C. Wragg*
EFFECTIVE TEACHING	*Richard Dunne and Ted Wragg*

Classroom Skills Series

Series editor
Clive Carré

ASSESSMENT AND LEARNING

Primary and Secondary

Ted Wragg

London and New York

First published 1997
by Routledge
11 New Fetter Lane, London EC4P 4EE

Simultaneously published in the USA and Canada
by Routledge
29 West 35th Street, New York, NY 10001

© 1997 Ted Wragg

Typeset in Palatino by
Solidus (Bristol) Limited
Printed and bound in Great Britain by
TJ International Ltd, Padstow, Cornwall

British Library Cataloguing in Publication Data

A catalogue record for this book is available from the British
Library

Library of Congress Cataloging in Publication Data

Wragg, E. C. (Edward Conrad)
        Assessment and learning / Ted Wragg.
            p.   cm. – (Classroom skills)
        Includes bibliographical references.
        1. Educational tests and
measurements.   2. Students–Rating of.
        3. Learning–Evaluation.   I. Title.   II. Series:
Classroom skills series.
        LB3051.W676   1997
        371.26–dc21   97–12955

ISBN 0-415-14342-X

CONTENTS

ASSESSMENT AND LEARNING

When 10-year-old Emma arrives at school one morning she meets her teacher in the playground. 'Did you finish *The Funfair of Evil* last night?' Mrs Jackson asks. Emma nods. 'Yes, I really enjoyed it.' 'Oh good,' Mrs Jackson smiles. 'Well done.'

This harmless-looking exchange is Emma's first assessment of the day. Her teacher is acknowledging that she has done last night's homework, which was to finish off the book she has been reading in class. Mrs Jackson's smile and words of approval are a signal that she has checked Emma's progress in an initial informal manner and is content at this stage. Later in the morning she may question Emma about the book, perhaps asking her to read from it, or Emma may have to write her own personal account of her reaction to what she has read. Both teacher and pupil may enter a statement in their respective record books that the book has been finished. Emma's record book may already contain a statement from her mother confirming that she read the book at home.

This routine set of events contains several mini-assessments, some informal, some formal. Children learn in different ways and at various times, so their assessment needs to reflect that diversity. When the teacher asks Emma about the book she has read and hears her read, this is a simple oral test. Writing down in a small booklet or a teacher's notebook some statements about the pupil's progress by the teacher, the parent and the pupil herself are the 'record keeping' part of the assessment. Emma was given a standardised reading test at the beginning of the year which showed that she is about average for her age, and this too was recorded, but the daily informal transactions are far more numerous than the less frequent formal tests. Assessment in school is a rich mixture of styles and purposes.

A few years ago I knew a secondary head teacher who boasted proudly that he had never assessed a pupil in his life. Yet he often wrote references for his school leavers, and on many occasions I saw him asking questions. He frequently offered words of approval to those who had done something that brought credit to the school, and I once witnessed him getting very cross with a pupil who had carelessly thrown a piece of litter in the school yard, telling him off and ordering him to pick it up. What he presumably meant was that he did not attach much importance to written examinations, but whether he liked the idea or not, he was assessing pupils' social and intellectual progress and behaviour every day.

There are many ways in which teachers evaluate their pupils' progress. Most of the day-to-day transactions are frequent and *informal* – a smile, a corrected spelling, a frown, a word of praise, a reprimand, a question asked to an individual, a group, or the whole class. Some are *semi-formal*, like a class test at the end of a week or study unit, while others are *formal*, like national tests given to 7-, 11- and 14-year-olds, or examinations for school pupils, university and college students.

There are many *purposes* that lie behind assessment. Most often the principal purpose is to give feedback to teacher and pupil, so that each knows what has been learned and what is not yet understood. Sometimes the purpose behind an assessment may be to select or assign some pupils rather than others to certain classes or facilities. This happens when children are selected for a particular school on the basis of an examination; when their special educational needs are assessed;

or when certain ones are picked for school sports teams, or to appear in drama and music presentations.

There are also numerous means of assessing progress. The commonest formal methods are familiar to anyone who has ever taken a test or completed a course: written exams, multiple-choice items, problem solving, oral and practical tests, assignments, projects, dissertations, work completed during the course. The technology of testing is highly developed and the testing industry is a multi-million-pound enterprise.

It would be easy to see assessment purely as something that teachers do to pupils on behalf of society, and nothing more. There is an important element of assessment here which cannot and should not be ignored. Society often does need to know what its members have learned, especially where people are selling their services to their fellows. None of us would want to be operated on by an amateur surgeon, or have the brakes on our car repaired by an enthusiastic ignoramus. We like to believe that someone has accredited these professionals on our behalf, formally checking out their knowledge and skill, so that their certificate of qualification ensures that they are competent. The long process of appraising knowledge, skill and competence begins early in children's lives.

While the formal evaluation of pupils' progress is an important part of this book, another vital purpose is to relate assessment to learning. From time to time teachers may indeed be required to make an 'official' statement about what their pupils have learned, showing the evidence for their evaluation, but most assessment is directly related to pupils' learning, especially that which gives feedback about their progress and needs. This means that the daily routines of assessment need to be carried out just as carefully and thoughtfully as the three-hour written examination paper. Since many judgments exercised on a day-to-day basis have to be made at speed by teachers caught up in a myriad of classroom transactions, it is important to reflect on the whole issue of assessment away from the rapidly changing hurly-burly of the classroom.

This book is intended to offer teachers a means of reflecting on assessment and then taking action to improve teaching and learning in their own classrooms. That is why it uses a combination of text and 'activity boxes'. It is certainly not meant to be a complete text on its own. There are numerous good books on different aspects of assessment, some of which go into great detail about particular aspects, like how to construct a test, the measurement of standards over time, statistical matters. Most tend to address formal, rather than informal, means of assessment, whereas in this book I have tried to cover both. A further broad intention is to refer the reader not only to the implications of assessment on pupils' learning, but also to the possibility of pupils being involved in it themselves, for self-evaluation is often omitted from books on assessment.

There are many additional books that can be consulted by readers wanting more detail on specific aspects of assessment. Broad-ranging texts addressing the main elements have been written by several authors, including Becker and Engelmann (1976), Beggs and Lewis (1975), Gronlund (1985) and Satterly (1981). Some writers have laid out the main issues specifically for a teacher audience. These include Desforges (1989), Frith and Macintosh (1984), Gipps (1990) and Harris and Bell (1990).

Other books give more detail on important aspects of assessment. Broadfoot (1987) has described how pupil profiling can be used. Ashworth (1982) and Green (1963) show how teachers can construct their own tests, while Ebel (1965) has written one of the classic texts on test construction. Goldstein and Lewis (1996) have collected a set of authoritative chapters by different writers with a strong emphasis on statistical and methodological issues, and Levy and Goldstein (1984) have assembled a series of critical reviews of many of the commonly used tests. The national and international issue of comparing standards between groups or monitoring achievement over a period of time, a common topic for political debate, has been addressed in a collection of articles written by experts in various fields, edited by Boyle and Christie (1996). Bibliographic details of all these works can be found in the References section at the end of this book.

There are six units in this book:

Unit 1 investigates the manifold nature of assessment, showing how different forms are used in schools, including informal and formal means.

Unit 2 considers the major principles and purposes of assessment, including the important matters of validity and reliability, as well as diagnosis, selection and prediction.

Unit 3 describes some of the many informal

methods that teachers employ, such as question and answer during classroom interaction, interview and observation.

Unit 4 deals with formal methods, like written tests (both teacher-constructed and commercially produced), the various subject contexts, marking and checking.

Unit 5 covers assessment in various subjects, the important matter of self-assessment, which empowers pupils to evaluate their own work, and the marking, recording and where necessary reporting of assessment.

Unit 6 concentrates on a 'whole school' approach, discussing how schools can develop effective policies and practice, including the issue of staff development, school inspection, teacher appraisal and the use of league tables to compare schools.

HOW TO USE THIS BOOK

It is possible for individuals or groups to work their way through this book, with or without a tutor or mentor, but there is great benefit for either experienced or novice teachers to work collaboratively with others on some of the activities. There is nothing more beneficial to a school than a feeling that all are working together to improve their individual and collective competence.

The *text* can simply be read in its own right by those wanting to reflect on assessment, or work alone on improving their own knowledge and skill in the field.

The *'activity'* sections are of different kinds, involving discussion, writing, or some kind of practical task. There are many ways in which these can be used for individual or group development:

- *Discussion activities* can be undertaken by trainee or experienced teachers, or by the two groups working together, for it is of benefit to both beginners and seasoned practitioners to explore the fresh and experienced views of professional competence.
- *Written activities*, like noting thoughts on a topic, can be done by individuals, but also by groups. They can be discussed orally when they have been completed.
- *Practical activities*, such as constructing, giving and marking a test, are designed to be undertaken by teachers either in their own classroom or as experiments with small groups of children or with individuals. These can easily be modified to suit the subject matter, or the age group, background, interests and abilities of the pupils concerned.

The written and discussion activities provide ideas for about 1 to 1½ hours of work, sometimes less. The practical activities usually require a shorter amount of time in the actual classroom, but can easily take a similar 1 to 1½ hours of work for follow-up.

THE MANIFOLD NATURE OF ASSESSMENT

Trying to assemble a log of all the occasions when children are assessed during a school day, week or year would soon produce a very full dossier. All the following are arguably different forms of assessment:

- A child shows the teacher a finished painting; the teacher says 'Well done!' and puts it up on the classroom wall.
- The teacher asks the class, 'What is the capital of France?'
- Three pupils work together in a physical education lesson to improve each other's gymnastic ability.
- The teacher sets a spelling test.
- A pupil takes her technology project to the teacher, who points out how the finish of it could be improved.
- At the end of their course several classes take a public examination in mathematics lasting two hours.
- A group of pupils performs a short play in front of the class, followed by a discussion of their performance by teacher and pupils.
- A teacher reprimands a pupil for misbehaving and says, 'If you do that again you'll stay in during break.'
- The head teacher asks two pupils with particularly good singing voices if they would like to sing a duet at the town's music festival.
- A teacher grades a student's portfolio of coursework for a public examination, prior to its being assessed by an external moderator.

Although these examples may be given the umbrella caption 'assessment', they are quite different from each other. Some are formal, like the maths exam, others are informal, like the smile and subsequent display of the child's painting. There are examples of academic achievement being assessed, as in the coursework moderation, but also instances of social behaviour being appraised, as in the case of the pupil threatened with detention for misbehaviour. Some evaluation is external, like the public examination, most other examples are internal to the school, or a mixture of internal and external.

The assessment is mainly carried out by teachers, but some examples illustrate self-evaluation, like the three children improving each other's gymnastics. The maths exam comes at the end of the pupils' maths course and so is 'summative' or 'terminal' (though hopefully not in the 'fatal' sense of the word), whereas the teacher suggesting how the girl can improve her technology project is carrying out a 'formative' or 'interim' assessment, which can still influence the pupil's finished product.

Already you can see some of the considerable differences between the many forms of assessment available to teachers. Standardised tests may have cost millions to develop over a period of a year or more. Home-made tests may have consumed hours of the teacher's time to construct, as may the marking of pupils' coursework. A smile, a nod, a threat of punishment, may occupy a few seconds of the teacher's and pupil's time. Any of these may make a significant impact on children's learning, for good or ill.

The consequences of each form of assessment may also be very different. Some, like public examination results or selection tests, may affect career choices, opportunities, someone's whole future. Others may appear to have had little or no influence on learning and subsequent behaviour. The two pupils selected by the head for their good singing voices may one day feel encouraged to specialise in the performing arts, since they are 'officially' thought to be good at them. Both positive and negative consequences may follow different kinds of assessment, depending on the personality of the recipient. Some pupils may be motivated by a critical assessment and strive to improve, others may feel demolished by it and simply erect a block against the subject, topic or teacher. One evaluation may be 'redeemable', in that pupils can subsequently improve their grade, while another might apply a permanent label, unless the candidate takes the whole course again.

TYPES OF ASSESSMENT

The dimensions below are presented as pairs of opposites, but in practice most teachers use some form of both types, as well as hybrid variants in between. The issues described under each of the headings are closely linked one with another, rather than separated.

Formal or informal?

No one form of assessment can suit all conceivable purposes and locations. If society decides to find out whether standards of reading amongst thousands of primary pupils have risen or fallen, then this sort of information cannot be gleaned solely by holding occasional conversations with individual teachers, illuminating though that exercise may be. A more formal assessment of achievement, or gleaning of collective judgements, would be necessary. On the other hand, if a teacher wants to know whether children have understood her instructions about what clothing to bring for a school trip, the easiest and most natural approach is informal – simply to ask them, as a group or as individuals.

In most classrooms, assessment tends to be regular and informal, rather than irregular and formal. This is because teaching often consists of frequent switches in who speaks and who listens, and teachers make many of their decisions within one second (Wragg, 1994). In such a rapidly changing environment, where teachers have to think on their feet and are denied the luxury of hours of reflection over each of their pedagogic choices, assessment has to be carried out on the move. That is why so much informal assessment is interlaced with instruction and activity, often barely perceptible as the flow of the lesson

continues. Indeed, many teachers would not even regard the common question, 'Is anybody not sure what you're supposed to do?' as assessment, but it is, informing the teacher of which pupils might need individual help before starting on the task in hand.

This last example illustrates some of the strengths and weaknesses of informal assessment. Asking a question to the class is a natural event and economical of time, but some pupils may be reluctant to put up their hand and risk revealing their ignorance to their fellows. Once children are working on their assignment, it is common practice for teachers to walk round monitoring what they are doing. Sometimes this kind of informal assessment will reveal that a pupil who was reluctant to put up his hand and ask for help in a public way is in fact struggling with the work and does need assistance. There are many forms of informal assessment available to teachers, both public and semi-private, and one approach may be more effective than another in a particular set of circumstances.

Formal assessment is usually much more structured than informal approaches. Sometimes it will involve a standardised test, an examination paper, or assessment schedule drawn up by an external body. There are normally written statements about how the assessment must be carried out, laying down how much time is available, what questions must be addressed, where the scripts or projects are to be sent afterwards. 'Formal' here does not mean 'unpleasant', or 'threatening', though these adjectives may sometimes apply, but rather that the exercise is governed by a predetermined set of rules and conventions, instead of being improvised according to immediate circumstances.

An example of the differences between informal and formal methods can be seen in the field of modern language teaching. During the oral part of a German lesson the teacher may put questions in the foreign language to individuals or groups. If several pupils mispronounce the sound 'ch', as in the German word *Kirche* (meaning 'church'), this informal assessment tells her that she will need to help them practise the correct pronunciation. Later in the lesson she may walk round looking at their written work, noticing that some pupils make mistakes when writing in the past tense. This signals that some revision and corrective work will be necessary if they are to use the past tense properly in future.

Informal assessment – checking on progress

Formal assessment – supervising a standardised test

A formal assessment, however, might involve all the pupils in the class being tape-recorded, one at a time, for several minutes, answering a series of predetermined questions. They may subsequently sit in an examination room and write answers in German. Both cassettes and written scripts may then be sent away for marking. It is also possible to have a semi-formal version of assessment, perhaps with the teacher devising and then administering a simple pencil and paper test of vocabulary that pupils have recently learned, or playing a pre-recorded cassette of German dialogue and asking pupils to write down answers to questions. This is formal, in that it follows certain rules and conventions, but informal, as it is given at a suitable moment in class and barely interrupts the flow of normal teaching.

The strengths and weaknesses of varying degrees of formality are fairly clear. Teaching is a busy job, so informality can offer natural, unfussy and frequent ways of gauging progress, offering feedback, or eliciting the sort of diagnostic information that informs teachers what logical next steps might be taken. It may, however, be too *ad hoc* and improvised to give a proper picture, and it may not always provide the degree of reflective objectivity necessary to counterbalance excessive subjectivity. Formal assessment may allow comparison with others, opportunities to measure improvement in a systematic way, and also, at its best, rigorously tested and considered instruments of assessment, but may overawe the less confident pupils, or give an incomplete picture of what they have been doing over a long period.

Continuous or final?

It is again a feature of many courses in school that pupils are assessed along the way and also that they receive some kind of assessment at the end of their course. Continuous assessment is often thought to be good for pupils who are more anxious than their fellows, but Child (1977) points out that this can depend on the nature of the tasks, as pupils faced with a series of appraisals they cannot manage particularly well, may become demoralised.

One central concept in teaching and learning is that of *motivation*. As will be discussed again in Unit 2, to some extent 'motivation' can be defined in operational terms as the amount of time and the degree of what psychologists call 'arousal' that pupils apply to their learning. If motivation is high, then children will spend a great deal of time and give much attention to what they are doing. Over a period of weeks and months this ought to make a difference to their achievement in the field of study, provided the programme is well conceived and worthwhile. Continuous assessment, by offering regular feedback, may help maximise concentration and attentiveness. If it is seen by pupils in a negative light, however, it may reduce time and effort spent on the programme of study.

Some of the same points about motivation can be made in the context of final or terminal assessment. Those who support end-of-course examinations argue that many pupils would not do as much work were there not some 'official' grade or certificate to strive for at the conclusion of the whole programme, and that this outweighs the more taken-for-granted continuous assessment.

It certainly does seem to be the case that a number of pupils will be spurred on by *extrinsic* motivation, that is external rewards, like good test grades. Others respond better to *intrinsic* motivation, something being seen to be worthwhile in its own right. Where continuous assessment contributes to the final overall grade, it is much more similar, in its external importance and the way it may be perceived, to final assessment. Adult life is often driven by a mixture of both extrinsic (e.g. salary or status) and intrinsic (e.g. personal satisfaction) motivation and rewards.

Coursework or examination?

Many systems of public examination consist of a mixture of continuous and terminal assessment. The national grading of 7-, 11- and 14-year-olds is based on both an end-of-phase examination and a teacher's assessment derived from a more sustained evaluation of children's progress. However, teacher and test grades are awarded at the end of a phase lasting two or more years, so the teacher element is not, strictly speaking, 'coursework', but rather an end-of-course evaluation influenced by close first-hand observation and evaluation of the child's work over a period of time.

General Certificate of Secondary Education and A level exams, by contrast, often have a coursework element which is accumulated throughout two years of study, perhaps a portfolio of artwork, essays, logbooks or projects. In the case of modular examinations, there will usually be formal grading of these at intervals throughout the course. Modular examinations are sometimes controversial when students can retake modules and try to improve their grade. People used to the traditional 'one-shot' exam find this odd, as it embodies a different concept, the appraisal of competence in a non-competitive way. The driving test is a long-standing example of an assessment that can be taken as many times as the candidate wishes. The issue there is whether someone is safe to be let loose on the roads, not what level of competence they reached in competition with others, or how long it took them.

One major concern when coursework and examinations are discussed is the matter of security and integrity. Badly monitored coursework is open to abuse, especially in the form of *plagiarism*, that is, passing off someone else's work as your own. Plagiarism is usually regarded as a serious offence when it is detected, and is frequently a reason for disqualifying candidates from the exam, or, in some cases, debarring them from future entry. Formal examinations supervised and patrolled in exam halls are not totally immune from cheating either, and again the penalties are usually severe.

Coursework must be carefully monitored for it to be taken seriously. The issue for society is very much concerned with the integrity of the award on offer. Can citizens put their trust in it? Have electricians, plumbers, doctors, teachers been

'My dad used to do all my homework'

licensed to practise on the basis of their own, rather than somebody else's, work and competence? This concern applies equally to non-vocational qualifications and other kinds of formal test where the results may one day play a part in the public domain, for example, be a part of a candidate's application for a job.

The difficulty comes when children have quite legitimately been encouraged to seek help from parents and other adults, especially in the early years of education. Learning as a family, rather than solitary, activity has been stressed for some decades, particularly since the Plowden Report (1967) on primary education, and research quoted within it (Young and McGeeney, 1968) stressed the important role that parents could play in their children's progress. The dilemma about what constitutes legitimate help at home is shared by parents themselves, often uncertain whether any contribution they might make is too much or too little. In many homes of people working in the professions there are considerable resources, such as books, equipment, CD ROMs, videos, even international databases, as well as the extensive knowledge of the parents themselves. Advice and school policy on such matters will be addressed again in Unit 6.

Fear of plagiarism, however, should not deter teachers from assessing coursework. Checking out that someone's work is their own is frequently done by oral cross-questioning about the subject matter, whether this is a piece of homework in the primary school, or a *viva voce* examination for a doctorate. Adult life is often more like coursework than formal examination, especially in the field of work. It is much more likely that employees will have to work at a task or a project over a sustained period of time, than that they will be asked to sit down and answer a test paper.

Nonetheless, most people have to be able to recall information, or demonstrate their knowledge and skill instantaneously, at some time or other. Formal examinations may be unreal in daily life, but if well conceived, they do offer the opportunity to check pupils' own learning and their ability to apply it. If the results of coursework and examination evaluation are fed back to children, then both can be valuable sources of information for future learning.

Written or oral?

There are two considerations when written and oral assessments are being undertaken. The first is the nature of the knowledge or skills being appraised. If certain aspects of subject areas such as spoken language in the first or second language, musical performance, or drama are being assessed, then it might in any case be more valid to test these orally.

The second issue is related to purpose, time and feasibility. If a semi-permanent record is required that can be studied, analysed and consulted again on future occasions, by teacher or pupil, then written work may be more useful than sets of cassettes, videos, or recourse to memory. If the assessment is informal and immediate, then it is often best tackled as a natural part of oral classroom discourse: a question and answer, a comment from the teacher, an explanation from a pupil with a teacher's response. Equally, however, very rapid written responses can be obtained: a short written statement from pupils, a quick pencil and paper test, a few multiple-choice items.

Individual or group?

Most formal assessment tends to be of the work of individuals, and most records are kept under the name of each pupil separately. Much of the time

this makes good sense: children are different from each other in their speed of learning, the amount of work they put in, the degree of knowledge and skill they acquire. It seems only right, therefore, to keep personal records of each child in the class, especially as the day will come when they have to take public examinations, apply for jobs, or seek entry to further or higher education as individuals, and will be judged on their own proficiency, not that of others.

On some occasions children actually work in a team, and their work may need to be assessed on either an individual or a group basis. Examples include: a drama improvisation or production; a team sporting event; a choir or small vocal or instrumental group; a technology project with different aspects in the hands of different pupils; two or three pupils conducting science experiments together; a class or group newspaper, portfolio or video; a group survey or investigation; a field project in geography or biology.

If such team projects are assessed, then teachers face a dilemma. Offer a single grade and some pupils may resent the fact that they worked hard for the same mark as someone else who was a parasite, or may be cross that their own higher quality contribution was recorded at a lower level because of someone else's poorer work. Award a series of individual marks, and pupils may bicker about why some members of the team scored more highly than others.

Group assessment often builds in statements about the particular contribution of each member (e.g. in the case of a video, who took responsibility for planning, scripting, camera work, editing, captions, graphics, sound, lighting). Sometimes there may be individual elements as well as a whole group submission, in which case teachers need to be careful that they do not overemphasise the more easily assessed individual components and lose sight of the contribution people have made to the whole project. In some cases teachers invite pupils to make a self-assessment, a perfectly legitimate strategy, but one which must also be handled with extreme care. Young pupils sometimes have little experience on which to base a critical self-evaluation, and adolescents are often afraid of appearing to sponsor themselves in case it is at the expense of their colleagues. Group assessments are not easy to carry out, but so much of adult life consists of teamwork that it would be a pity if the difficulties ruled them out.

What is assessed?

Irrespective of what methods are used, there are so many aspects of learning on which to focus that it would take a much longer book than this to describe them fully. Some of the main aspects include the following, with a few examples:

Knowledge and understanding   Factual information, concepts, names, labels, ideas, theories, applications, connections, analogies, relationships, structures, beliefs.
Skills   Techniques, mental and physical dexterity, specific competence in particular fields, craft expertise, interpersonal skills, the ability to link knowledge, understanding and skill.
Attitudes and values   About learning, behaviour, beliefs, subject knowledge, people, society.
Behaviour   Social relationships, personal characteristics, competence at carrying something out, fulfilling potential.

Take a field such as 'health education' in general and 'diet and exercise' in particular. In order to assess how effectively a child had learned about leading a healthy life, it would be possible to try and assess each of the four areas mentioned above, namely *knowledge and understanding* (e.g. what is known about physical and mental health, healthy and unhealthy foods, diseases that can be avoided, understanding the need for at least three periods of twenty minutes per week of vigorous exercise to reduce the risk of heart disease), *skills* (e.g. knowing how often and also being able to perform a range of activities and exercise that help avoid conditions likely to cause disease), *attitudes* (e.g. does the pupil have a positive or negative attitude towards regular exercise and a healthy diet?), and *behaviour* (e.g. do pupils actually eat a healthy diet and take exercise?).

Some of these areas are easier to assess than others. Particular pieces of knowledge and concepts are often easier to appraise than attitudes, or children's behaviour out of school, or influences on their eventual lifestyle once they have left altogether. That is why many of the more elaborate assessment schemes combine oral and written tests, interviews, observations, rating scales and personal profiles.

ACTIVITY 1

Many forms of assessment

1   Take a particular school subject, like mathematics, English, science, or history, and consider which aspects of it might be assessed according to some of the precepts raised in this unit, like the use of oral questioning, formal examinations, practical tests, continuous assessment, etc. Consider in particular the likely effect of each of these approaches on pupils' learning.
2   Discuss a *cross-curricular theme* like health education, and consider, as above, the different approaches that might be used in the assessment of pupils' progress, and the possible effects of each of these on children's learning.

PITFALLS IN ASSESSMENT

Even carefully conceived forms of assessment may go awry from time to time, so some of the possible pitfalls must be faced from the beginning. Many of the issues mentioned below will recur throughout this book.

Validity

Not all forms of assessment are valid, in that they do not always measure what they are supposed to measure. An example would be a written test of knowledge in a subject like science for very young children who had not yet learned to read and write proficiently. The results would reflect achievement in language rather than science.

Reliability

There are many forms of 'reliability' to consider, and this topic and that of 'validity' are covered in greater detail in Unit 2. A badly conceived assessment may fail the validity test, by not measuring what it was supposed to measure, but it may also be unreliable. For example, it might be scored differently by different markers, or give different results on different occasions.

Self-fulfilling prophecy

If assessment is seen by pupils as the final word on their competence, then they may believe they are limited in what they can achieve, and simply close their minds to further learning, or perform at a level below their capabilities. It can be especially hard for younger children to refute a label, as they have little with which to compare themselves and may be heavily influenced by what adults say about them. From the teacher's standpoint, it may lead to stereotyping, whereby pupils are automatically categorised as certain types of achiever, rather than being freshly assessed each time.

Consequences

All assessments have outcomes, and these may be beneficial or innocuous, so this 'pitfall' is more about unintended or unnoticed consequences. Premature labelling has already been mentioned above, but too little or too much assessment, for example, might lead to a subsequent loss of motivation. Children who never receive feedback on their work, or who are tested too frequently, may lose interest.

Measuring the measurable

Assessment may concentrate too much on what is easily measured, instead of what is important. In music, for example, it is far more simple to give a written test to see whether pupils know what 'andante' means than it is to assess more diffuse and elusive notions such as 'love of music' or 'understanding'. Yet many music teachers hope that the children they teach will show a lifelong interest in listening to and making music. It would be a pity if assessment concentrated entirely or substantially on what is straightforward and ducked anything problematic.

International comparisons

International comparisons based on tests of achievement are given great prominence in the mass media, the assumption being that some international league table of academic achievement captures the essence of a country's success or failure. The problems in international comparisons are of many kinds. The first is that it is extremely difficult in any comparison to draw up parallel samples. Some countries have a selective system and others do not, so certain samples may be overweighted with above- or below-average pupils.

Another difficulty is that countries like Germany practise 'grade retention', that is, hold back pupils who perform badly and require them to repeat the year. A sample of 'third year pupils', therefore, might include low-achieving fourth years, but exclude low-achieving third years, as they have been kept back in the second year.

A third pitfall is that some international tests favour countries that cover a narrow curriculum and penalise those that roam broadly, as they are drawn up to reflect the topics that are common to most countries' curricula. Thus in mathematics there is often great emphasis on 'number', but less on 'probability and statistics'. Most international comparisons have been done in mathematics (e.g. Postlethwaite, 1987; Burghes and Blum, 1995), and the results often generalised by the mass media not only to the whole of mathematics, but to the whole of education. McLean (1996) has summarised international studies in a number of fields.

Politicisation

Education spends large amounts of public money, so it is bound to come under public scrutiny. One problem, however, is that the assessment of pupils' progress and learning becomes a political issue, especially when the ruling party tries to defend its record and opposition parties attack it, though in the 1980s and 1990s in Britain it was sometimes the party in power that criticised pupil achievement.

An example of the politicisation of assessment occurs in the use of league tables of test results to compare one school with another, a practice based on the belief that competition foments improvement. The accurate measurement of change is especially difficult in education, because it is not usually possible to match groups of pupils exactly in a controlled experiment, nor is it possible to hold several factors constant throughout a year to investigate the effect, say, of teaching styles or skills on one particular outcome, like pupil learning.

The significant correlation that exists between such factors as social background and educational achievement begins at an early age (Davie, Butler and Goldstein, 1972), so league tables of raw unadjusted test scores often reflect the differences in abilities amongst the pupils, rather than the effects of skilful or unskilful teaching.

Alternatives to raw score league tables, none of which is entirely satisfactory, will be discussed again in Unit 6. The question of politicisation raises the matter of the principles and purposes of assessment, and this is the central focus of Unit 2.

 ACTIVITY 2

League tables

1 Consider this league table of schools' performance according to three criteria: the average percentage of pupils absent each day without due cause (truants), the percentage who obtain five or more high-grade GCSEs, the average rating per pupil of behaviour in class (on a five-point scale, given by an observer).

	Truancy (%)	High-grade GCSE (% with 5 A–C)	Pupil behaviour (average rating)
School A	2.4	32.4	3.2
School B	1.2	43.2	4.1
School C	4.3	26.8	2.6
School D	0.6	13.4	4.5
School E	4.6	45.3	3.1

2 Think about, or discuss with others, the following:

Type of assessment What sort of features are being assessed, and how important do you think they are to teachers, parents, employers, society at large, the pupils themselves?

Ease of assessment How easy or difficult is it to assess each of the features, such as unauthorised absence, GCSE grades, pupils' social behaviour?

Conclusions What conclusions do you draw from the tables, and how confident do you feel about each of them? Do the figures conform to a pattern, or are there anomalies? What further information might you need in order to make judgements?

Effects What do you think the positive and negative effects on the school might be of publishing tables in this form? Are there different ways of displaying the data? What might be the effect of publishing the average number of high-grade (A to C) GCSE results per pupil, rather than percentage of pupils who obtained five high grades?

PRINCIPLES AND PURPOSES OF ASSESSMENT

There is little point in being armed with a battery of assessment strategies if they are based on shaky principles and unclear purposes. Principles and purposes are closely intertwined. The best techniques available are useless if the validity and reliability of the approaches and instruments being used are suspect, and this applies as much to informal assessment as it does to formal means. If a teacher concluded, without checking, that a child must have understood the point she had made, as he had just smiled, then this might turn out to be an invalid assessment. Children smile for different reasons, including both comprehension and bewilderment.

PRINCIPLES OF ASSESSMENT

Validity and reliability are amongst the most important precepts in evaluation. There are several forms of both of them, as each is not just a single concept, and they are related to each other, even though they are often dealt with under separate headings. They are not, however, the only considerations, and other principles will also be addressed in this unit.

Validity

The central question asked when the validity of any form of assessment is being scrutinised, however formal or informal it may be, is this:

Does the assessment measure what it purports to measure?

Face validity

For most informal day-to-day forms of regular appraisal, face validity is the most common criterion. In other words, does it *look* as if it does the job it is intended to do? The two items below both appear to have face validity: (a) checks whether children can convert a fraction to a decimal and vice versa, while (b) examines whether someone knows when the Victorian era took place.

(a) Turn the decimal 6.75 into a fraction. What is 3¼ in decimals?
(b) In what year was Queen Victoria born? When did she become queen? When did she die?

However, it would soon be possible to reduce the validity of both these items. To some extent all questions, written or oral, are a test of language, as well as of the subject matter being taught, so many-faceted assessment is inescapable. Subject matter assessment is bound to include language knowledge, and so it should, since language is the principal means through which we communicate. Indeed, learning to use and understand the appropriate terminology is often a significant aspect of learning the subject. But the addition of more complex language to the maths problem (a), for example, by using words like 'Convert the expression …' instead of the more simple 'Turn …', pushes the item further down the 'language' test track. Consideration of face validity involves deciding the main focus of an assessment, however informal.

In the case of (b), adding the question 'For how many years was she queen?' would introduce a test of mathematical competence for those young children who had never been told the answer, but had to calculate the sum 1901–1837. Since she was actually queen for 63 years and seven months, subtracting June 1837 from January 1901 would shift the item even further towards a test of skill in maths. There is nothing wrong with combining more than one focus of assessment, but careful thought must be given to what is supposed to be the principal focus, as well as to its face validity, in the framing of written or oral questions. It is not always as simple a matter as it looks on the surface.

Content validity

This is a similar notion to face validity, but it raises the specific question: 'Does the assessment appear to reflect the content of the course?' If pupils have spent a week, a term, or a year studying a subject or a series of topics, then what they have covered should be reflected in the assessment. If they have studied electricity and magnetism, for example, then both topics should be included in their assessment.

This issue comes up in a similar context when the weighting of different components of an assessment is being decided. Pupils often complain, if they have spent three quarters of the time on 'electricity' and a quarter on 'magnetism', when their eventual assessment appears to concentrate more on the latter than the former.

Concurrent validity

There are often choices of approach available when evaluation of children's learning takes place. If a teacher wants to know how proficient a reader a particular pupil is, then a test may be given, or the child may read from a book, or perhaps be given a passage to read silently before being asked questions about its meaning. 'Concurrent validity' is the extent to which the form of assessment being used gives similar results when compared with other ways of assessing the same kind of knowledge, skill, or understanding.

When new standardised tests of achievement are compiled, the draft version is usually given to a sample of pupils along with other existing tests in the same subject area. The simplified hypothetical scores below would show high concurrent validity between the new test and 'Old test' A, but low compared with 'Old test' B.

	New test	Old test A	Old test B
Pupil 1	65	62	49
Pupil 2	81	79	50
Pupil 3	43	39	52
Pupil 4	55	51	56
Pupil 5	73	68	47

These differences may be explained in many ways. Perhaps Old test A is a test of 'factual knowledge', like the new test, while Old test B is more a measure of 'attitude to the subject', so they are attempting to assess different aspects of learning. Of course, if the new test assessed exactly what the old test measured, there would be no point in having it, so perfect matches are unlikely to occur.

One example of concurrent validity in the somewhat diffuse field of 'creativity' would be whether those people who scored highly on a written 'creativity' test were in fact 'creative' in real life. Did they invent things, come up with unusual solutions, exercise their imagination during their daily lives? Or did the test simply measure verbal fluency, rather than genuine creativity? In school assessment an example of concurrent validity would be if there were close agreement between a national test of children's ability in reading, writing or 'number', and teachers' estimates of their performance in these fields based on daily observation.

Predictive validity

Sometimes assessment is part of a prediction about the future, especially in the case of selection, where the assessment is used to make an estimate of who is most likely to be suitable for a higher or lower ability group, or who might undertake a particular assignment, like playing the lead in a dramatic performance, or reporting a group's activities back to the class. 'Mock exams', which schools usually schedule a few months before public examinations like the GCSE and A levels, are a good example of a pre-test, one purpose of which is to make predictions about how well or badly pupils are likely to perform in the real examination.

A significant period of time elapses before pupils take the public examination, and their 'mock' results offer feedback and possibly give them motivation to work harder, so one would not expect perfect agreement between the dress rehearsal and the real event. However, in the references they write for students applying for

'Oh yes, she's highly creative'

jobs, or for entry to further and higher education, teachers have to predict the grades they estimate the candidates will achieve. A mock exam with poor predictive validity, possibly because it was conceived differently from the real test, would be of little help in these circumstances.

Reliability

'Reliability' can also be considered under several headings, but all of them are largely about *consistency*. However, unless an assessment has validity there is little point in even considering its reliability, for the notion 'reliable, but invalid'

would be useless. It would simply mean that the assessment failed to measure what it was supposed to measure, but did so in a consistently inaccurate way, not exactly a recipe for success. Among several types of reliability commonly discussed are the ones below.

Pupil performance

Supposing you assessed a group of pupils one day, and could then wipe their memories clean of all traces of what had happened. If you used exactly the same kind of assessment the following day, would the results be the same? They would almost certainly not be exactly the same, even in this idealised fictitious experiment, partly because children change from one day to the next, and partly because no test is perfect.

Pupils might remember their answers, if exactly the same test were given again, so systematic checks on standardised tests often involve two parallel forms of the test, Form A and Form B, being given to the same sample on two occasions. The two sets of scores are then compared, in what is known as a 'test–retest' or 'parallel forms' correlation. The higher the correlation, the more consistent or 'reliable' a measure of pupil performance the test is thought to be. The same notion can be applied to informal assessment. One example would be checking whether oral questions are unambiguously worded, so that children are clear what they are being asked and would answer in the same way on another occasion, whereas ambiguous or badly phrased questions might obtain different answers.

Test construction

There are various ways of checking the *internal consistency* of any set of assessment items, whether these make up a single test or constitute a series of linked questions on the same topic. Many of these are quite complex to describe, as they involve special formulae.

The underlying principle is usually to check how far the items seem to be measuring the same factor. This can be carried out for each item separately, to see how well scores on it correlate with the scores pupils obtain on the total test. It can also be done by comparing one half of the items with the other half, for example, to elicit how well pupils have done on the even-numbered items compared with the odd-numbered ones. If the test is internally consistent, then there should be close agreement between scores on even- and odd-numbered questions. This is called a *'split half reliability'*.

Reliability in marking

Many factors can influence how people mark work they are assessing. They may have a particular mental set about individual pupils or a group, believing them to be industrious or lazy, clever or slow, conscientious or slipshod. This prejudgement may affect the grade they award, or lead to 'halo rating' (where most dimensions or items are given the same or a similar mark).

In one research project I undertook, teachers rated primary pupils' competence at reading and also their personality (e.g. whether they were 'determined' or 'gave in easily' when they encountered a difficulty). Pupils were also asked to rate themselves. There were high agreements between each of the scales on the teachers' ratings, and also between the various scales on the pupils' self-ratings. But there was no agreement between teachers' and pupils' scores. Both groups had engaged in 'halo rating'.

One way of checking the reliability of two markers is for each to assess the same work separately, award a grade or mark without telling the other, and not making any notes or comments on the scripts, if it is a written test. This is the so-called *'double blind'* approach. The marks can then be compared and the degree of agreement and disagreement ascertained and discussed. One difficulty with double blind marking, however, is that people may be tempted to cluster their marks close to the middle of the scale, so as not to be too far away from the other assessor. The *distribution* of marks must be discussed, as it is easy to obtain spurious agreement by scoring everything at or near the centre, a process known as 'central clustering', shown in the following table. This issue will be discussed again in Unit 4.

Pupil	Marker A	Marker B	Marker C
Ann	55	52	50
Charles	48	50	52
Eve	53	51	49
George	56	52	54
Janet	48	52	51

Central clustering **High-looking agreement between three markers, but all scores near the centre.**

Other principles

While validity and reliability are important principles, they are not the only concepts worth considering. It is possible to have highly valid and reliable assessments of something that is monumentally trivial or tedious and of no consequence. It would be possible to devise a valid and reliable assessment of children's ability to copy out telephone directories, but the activity would not be *worthwhile*. Consideration needs to be given, therefore, to what is actually worth assessing and recording, especially as so much time and energy can easily be spent by both teachers and pupils.

Another pragmatic matter for reflection is how *feasible* the assessment is. In an ideal situation, there would be vast amounts of time available for teachers to plan and carry out assessment. In reality there is often very little spare time and energy, and the whole process can easily be rushed and ill thought-out. Yet a great deal may be at stake for pupils and for the school, especially in the case of work that counts towards some significant external award. Making the best use of the time and resources available applies to both formal and informal assessment.

A further principle is what makes best sense in particular circumstances, the matching of assessment to purpose. There are many considerations. Two categories that are often discussed in this context are *norm-referenced* and *criterion-referenced* assessment. The first is founded on the notion of each person's relative place or ranking on a particular scale, the second on what someone can or cannot do.

Norm-referenced assessment

This is the form of assessment that places people in some kind of position on a scale of human achievement in a certain field. In other words, it compares them with the 'norm'. Many tests are constructed to spread pupils over a 'normal distribution', the bell-shaped curve that bulges in the middle, where most candidates are found, and thins out more and more at the extremes. In such a test, if the average mark is 50%, then most pupils will obtain between 40% and 60%. Few will gain a mark over 80% or below 20%.

Many types of formal assessment have been standardised on large samples, and the results translated into *percentiles*, so called because people have been divided into 100 equal groups, each called a percentile. This tells you where someone stands in relationship to others of the same age. Someone on percentile 2 would be one of the lowest achievers in the age group, whereas a person on percentile 98 would be one of the highest.

The pupil profiles below show the percentiles of two children on five different standardised measures. Ann is well above average in reading and has a very high degree of physical co-ordination, but is about average in maths and science. She is quite small for her age. Tim, by contrast, is tall compared with other children, but has poor co-ordination. His performance in reading is near the middle of the range, but he is quite a high achiever in maths and science.

	Reading	Maths	Science	Co-ordination	Height
Ann	84	54	53	96	19
Tim	48	73	82	12	71

Norm-referenced assessment can become self-fulfilling. For example, when standardised tests are constructed, items that do not produce a normal distribution may be discarded. Also the pupils, seeing themselves labelled in relation to their peers, may limit their own ambitions and some may make their 'averageness' come true.

At its best norm-referenced assessment, by letting teachers and pupils see where they stand, may spur them on to higher achievement. At its worst it may demoralise those labelled as being at or near the bottom. Furthermore, it does not set pupils objective standards, so a whole nation could find itself with low achievement levels, simply because it always constructed its own 'norms' and never looked outside. It may be better, in the words of the saying, to be a 'servant in heaven', rather than 'master in hell', but on a norm-referenced assessment, the servant in heaven would be on percentile 1, while the master in hell would sit proudly on percentile 100.

Criterion-referenced assessment

This form of assessment is based on a different principle. Instead of spreading people across a spectrum compared with others, it offers a list of criteria that have to be met. The driving test is a good example of this approach. If a candidate reversed into a lamp-post during the test, it would be futile to say, 'But I am on the 99th percentile when it comes to changing gear, emergency braking and knowledge of the highway code.' In order to be licensed to drive, you have to meet all the criteria in the test. You cannot compensate for poor performance in some aspects by brilliant achievement in others, as you might on a norm-referenced test.

Different principles are involved, so sometimes the procedures may differ from norm-referenced assessment. For example, in a norm-referenced test the time available may be strictly controlled, and only one attempt permitted. To give more time or a further attempt would breach the conditions under which the 'norms' had been determined. In theory, criterion-referenced tests are measuring whether or not someone can do

The driving test – a criterion-referenced test

something, so allowing a little extra time, or re-taking the test, makes little difference.

Criteria are usually listed in terms of what people should know or be able to do to obtain the award or to be given a particular grade or level. Syllabus statements are often expressed in 'can do' terms, like 'Can multiply two three-digit numbers', or 'Can convert a fraction to a decimal', or 'Knows the dates of all the English kings and queens from Queen Victoria to the present day'.

The differences between norm- and criterion-referenced tests are often exaggerated. Many norm-referenced tests contain criterion-referenced items. A maths test, for example, may consist of three additions, three subtractions, three divisions and three multiplications. Although the final score may be a mark out of twelve, it would often be possible to determine how well candidates could perform each of the four operations. Similarly,

criterion-referenced tests often make use of norm-referenced language, such as 'Reaches a reasonable level of …', 'Demonstrates a high degree of competence in …', or 'Shows a satisfactory grasp of …'. The words 'reasonable', 'high' and 'satisfactory' are often meant to be interpreted in terms of how others of a similar age or background might perform, so in that sense they too are norm-referenced.

a ACTIVITY 3

Validity and reliability

Discuss the different forms of validity and reliability described in this Unit as they might apply to commonly used forms of assessment like the four below, relating them to particular subjects, topics or age groups:

1   Essays of various kinds, or written accounts of what children have done.
2   Oral questioning of (a) individuals, (b) small groups, (c) the whole class.
3   Pencil and paper tests constructed by the teacher.
4   Standardised tests constructed by an external testing agency.

How can teachers balance a quest for the ideal against the pressures of time and energy?

PURPOSES OF ASSESSMENT

Many acts of assessment are related to a very specific purpose: a pupil has done some homework and wants feedback about it; the school is involved in a national testing programme; a child seeks entry to a school which has a competitive entrance examination. There are numerous categories into which various kinds of assessment can be fitted, including the following list, which is not exhaustive.

Knowledge of results (feedback)

Most learners are curious to know how effectively they have grasped some concept, principle, body of knowledge, or skill, so the reaction is sought of another, usually more knowledgeable person, able to comment on the accuracy or competence of what has been done. Some forms of interactive technology, like CD ROMs, offer feedback to responses. Feedback is sometimes seen as part of a behaviourist approach to learning, where it is part of the sequence 'stimulus–response–reinforcement'. It is, however, a feature of many approaches to teaching, and is often regarded as an essential adjunct to learning. Feedback is also seen as important for teachers, as it reveals what pupils appear to know or not to have learned, a matter taken up under the heading 'diagnosis' below.

Support and encouragement

Teachers sometimes use assessment to reveal to their pupils that progress is being made, and thereby to offer encouragement for further study in conjunction with a plan of action. This works well if pupils are on an improving curve of achievement. Some teachers even inflate their assessment in order to encourage, a practice that

is not always welcomed by the pupils themselves. The risk is that assessment may reveal little or no progress, and discourage students, hence the need for it to be handled judiciously. Assessment may even be used cynically to achieve the opposite, that is, to undermine and demoralise. This may be a comparative rarity in education, but it is not unknown in other fields, like initial training in the armed services and in some professional sports, where 'taking somebody down a peg' is more a part of the culture.

Motivation

Supporters of regular assessment often emphasise motivation as a main objective, arguing that pupils work harder if they know they are going to be assessed. As was described in Unit 1, motivation consists of time applied to the task and a degree of psychological arousal, so advocates of frequent assessment hope it will maximise the time and arousal that pupils bring to their work. Critics point to the dangers to motivation of repeated public or private failure, one of the potential pitfalls described earlier.

The motivational effects of assessment vary according to individuals and circumstances. Important formal examinations where much is at stake for the individual may well motivate many pupils, but equally some pupils will strive to answer questions in class, or be eager to reveal their knowledge and competence to their teacher. Others may be driven more by intrinsic motivation, so assessment may play only a minor role if they enjoy their study anyway.

Diagnosis

Some people dislike the term 'diagnosis' because of its medical associations and the implied assumption that children must be defective in some way. The word cannot be totally dry-cleaned of its other uses, but it should be perfectly possible, in education, to see it as meaning 'an appraisal of what might be done next, on the basis of what has been learned to date'. In this context it is benign, rather than deprecating.

Some tests are mainly designed for diagnostic purposes. A mark out of twenty on its own tells us relatively little about what children can and cannot do, unless teachers peruse every item on each test paper. A diagnostic profile, however, might reveal that a pupil can handle monosyllabic words, but not words of two or more syllables, or that he tends to guess at words largely by looking

Motivation – can assessment increase interest?

at their initial letter. This should put both teacher and pupil in a better position to move ahead. There is often a shortage of good diagnostic tests for specific subjects and topics, and so teachers may devise their own procedures.

Selection

This is a word with immense political significance. Yet assessment is often linked with selection, whether anyone likes it or not. Some pupils apply for entry to schools that have entrance tests; many schools have higher and lower sets based on ability in particular subject fields; children are picked for school teams, performances in concerts, parts in plays or other dramatic events; and teachers write references for former pupils who are applying for jobs. It may be done informally or semi-formally, but it exists.

There are two key concepts that cannot be ignored when assessment is linked to selection.

The first is 'fairness'. Children dislike teachers who are unfair (Wragg, 1994), and if they feel that a selection has been made on unfair grounds, this can leave a deep and long-lasting sense of resentment, which people are still able to recall and recount with bitterness well into adult life.

The second is 'labelling', an issue already mentioned above. Children have very little objective experience on which to base an assessment of their own abilities and achievement, beyond simple comparisons with their immediate fellows. What adults tell them can acquire considerable authority. Pupils repeatedly told they are not particularly good at a certain subject, or those never or rarely selected for some assignment, may simply block it in their minds in future and pay less attention when they are supposed to be studying it. Those labelled 'good', on the other hand, who are frequently rewarded with public selection, may feel a sense of success and buoyancy that increases or sustains their motivation. The inescapable dilemma for teachers is balancing the need for accurate, realistic and honest decisions, where selections have to be made, against the likely effects on the learner. Handling such matters with intelligence, sensitivity and integrity lies right at the heart of professional competence.

Measurement and comparison

Another controversial use of assessment is for purposes of comparison of individuals or groups. This is often seen as a central part of public accountability. One pupil, one class, one teacher, one school, one local authority, one country, or one particular year group, may be compared with others. The purpose of norm-referenced tests, for example, is to place a pupil at a point that has been determined by comparing large samples of children with one another.

The Assessment of Performance Unit, run by the Department of Education and Science in the 1970s and 1980s, compared samples of pupils in subjects like English and mathematics from one year to the next, in an attempt to elicit whether national standards of attainment were rising or falling. International comparisons of pupil achievement, as discussed in Unit 1, are undertaken to see how pupils in different countries compare.

One national survey (Foxman, Ruddock and McCallum, 1990) reported the scores of 11-year-olds in five areas of mathematics. In four areas, 'measures', 'geometry', 'algebra' and 'probability/statistics', the scores had gone up. In the fifth area, 'number', they had gone down. Not all press reports mentioned the improvements,

most concentrating on the decline in 'number'. In another study of mathematics achievement in seventeen different countries (Burghes and Blum, 1995), most press coverage drew attention to British 13-year-old pupils having done less well than German children in the field of 'number', rather than to their better performance in the field of geometry. It is important that such matters as good or poor performance in different subjects, or elements of them, should be brought to public attention, but anyone seriously concerned with knowing the full picture on national or international comparisons should read the original reports, rather than rely solely on press accounts.

a ACTIVITY 4

Principles and purposes

Choose a recent piece of assessment that you have undertaken, either a formal or an informal one. Ask yourself, or discuss with others, the following:

1. What was its principal purpose?
2. How was it conceived? Who decided it, what form did it take?
3. What was the outcome? How did children respond?
4. How did it help or hinder pupils' learning?
5. Would you carry it out in the same form in future, or alter it? If so, why and how? If not, why not?

INFORMAL METHODS OF ASSESSMENT

Books on assessment often describe only formal methods of assessment, giving most attention to those in written form, especially standardised tests. Yet most day-to-day assessment in primary and secondary classrooms is informal, frequently a seamless part of the process of teaching and learning. Over a period of time most teachers use a mixture of formal and informal methods. This unit will concentrate on informal methods and Unit 4 will cover more formal approaches.

Informal assessment can cover all the aspects of knowledge, understanding, skills, attitudes and behaviour that formal methods might address. In many ways it is easier, though still problematic, as an attempt can be made to check out pupils' knowledge or competence in a field where it might take weeks to devise a formal test. For example, trying to assess pupils' attitudes to social matters, to see whether they had changed over a period of time, would require a considerable effort via formally drawn-up attitude scales. Talking to pupils in class about their views may not be a perfect way forward, but it can give a valid picture of what they claim to believe. Similarly, studying their daily behaviour can help form a useful assessment of how their attitudes to social relationships manifest themselves in real life.

Informal assessment can be intuitive, undertaken on the spur of the moment, random, a response to whatever is the topic or theme at any particular time, and unrecorded. Equally it can be pre-planned, focused, and a record may be kept of it. A teacher of young children may hear a pupil read because she happens to notice the child looks baffled and may be finding that the book he is on is too difficult. She may also decide in advance to check the reading competence of a particular pupil by hearing her read from her current reader, later noting in her record book: 'Anna guesses words from the initial letter and tends not to look at the whole word.' Both are informal approaches, undertaken naturally as part of classroom interaction, but one is spontaneous and the other pre-planned.

Informal assessment can take place in a variety of settings and with very different purposes. The main focus may be on whether the pupil has understood a concept, acquired a piece of knowledge, learned a skill, is able to manifest a particular form of behaviour. The subject matter, activity or topic may also be influential on the form an informal evaluation takes.

Some fields are more straightforward than others. If a pupil in a maths lesson, when asked to answer the question $915 \div 3 = ?$, were to reply 35 instead of 305, then this would illustrate that he is making an elementary 'place value' error. He has failed to think through his answer in the proper hundreds, tens and units columns. There is a 'correct' textbook answer to the question and he has made a mistake that other pupils may also have made. Why he has made the error is a different and more difficult matter, but there is not much argument about the sum being wrong. There may, however, be plenty of argument about algorithms, methods of teaching and of assessment.

In other fields, by contrast, the rightness or wrongness of an answer may not be as clear-cut. A sum may be manifestly wrong, but assessing a painting, a poem, a belief, may not be as straight-forward, even if different evaluators can agree about some aspects of them. Yet it is just as important that fair and fruitful assessment should take place in fields where it may be more

Monitoring – have children understood?

difficult, otherwise it would appear that the only important human activities are those about which there is little or no doubt. In this unit we shall look, therefore, at a variety of informal assessments, not just those that are straightforward and unproblematic.

QUESTIONING

One of the most common forms of informal assessment is the use of oral questions. It is usual, during classroom discourse, for teachers to ask questions, whether these are put to individuals, small groups or the whole class. I have described the general use of questions more fully elsewhere (Wragg, 1993; Brown and Wragg, 1993), so I want to deal particularly here with questions that assess pupil learning.

Brown and Wragg (1993) described studies showing that about two-thirds of teachers' questions were designed to check knowledge and understanding, about half checked facts, and just over a half were intended to diagnose pupils' difficulties. Teachers may ask on average one, or even two, questions per minute, which means several hundred in a day and tens of thousands over a school year. If a half to two-thirds of these are connected in some way to assessment, then it is worth giving careful thought to how they can best be framed and what to do with pupils' answers, since classroom questioning represents a significant investment in time and energy.

There have been many classifications of teachers' questions. One simple division is between questions known as 'lower order' (recalling facts) and 'higher order' (recalling more than just facts). This is quite a crude distinction. The reproduction of some factual information can involve thinking of a very high order, for example if someone asked you to recall the formula of DNA. By contrast, the question 'Why is the centre of London noisier than the local morgue?' is in theory a 'higher order' question, as it requires the recall of information and then a minor piece of reasoning, yet it would not challenge the intellect too severely.

Assessing prior knowledge

When starting a new topic, teachers may use questions to assess what pupils know already. This diagnostic approach can provide valuable start-up information for teachers, revealing what

pupils do and do not know, or can and cannot do. Checking prior knowledge also offers a neat link between teacher assessment and subsequent pupil learning. It can be the first valuable step towards what is going to be learned in the future.

A student teacher I once observed had, with enormous care, prepared a lesson on volcanoes. She taught the first lesson by giving the class information about the nature of volcanoes: 'Today I want to tell you a little bit about volcanoes. Here is a model of one and you can see that this is the crater and, as you probably know, this is the lava, and this part here is called the magma chamber. Perhaps you've heard of volcanoes before. There's one in Italy called Vesuvius ...'

She was disappointed by the class's poor response on the rare opportunities she had given them to contribute. When she had a subsequent opportunity to teach the same topic to a similar group of pupils, she began by asking: '*What can you tell me about volcanoes?*' After a few hesitant responses, children began referring to television programmes, their friends' and parents' holiday and travel experiences, things they had read in books, mentioning Vesuvius, Etna, the dust from Krakatoa travelling several times around the Earth, craters on the moon, Icelandic geysers and various other notions, using terms like 'lava' and 'eruption'. This simple 'baseline assessment' question was the informal equivalent of a written 'pre-test'. It had given her a clearer insight into what various pupils already knew, so she was in a better position to capitalise on what she had learned.

Checking knowledge and understanding

Leaving aside the questions that are to do with class management, rather than the content of the lesson, studies of classroom interaction have shown that the majority of questions teachers ask, in both primary and secondary schools, do require the recall of factual information. However, if teachers are to check the state of pupils' knowledge of the relevant facts, and indeed their understanding of them, then the wording of questions is important, as is the nature of their response to pupils' answers.

Teachers' strategies may also be determined by the focus of the informal assessment. Is the principal purpose to check knowledge of facts, understanding of concepts, or both? Suppose the teacher wanted to check children's knowledge of facts about magnetism and also their understanding of the nature and practical application of the concept. The question: '*Does a magnet pick up objects made of copper?*' merely invites a 'yes' or 'no' response. Children who are guessing have a 50% chance of getting the correct answer.

It would probably take a battery of such questions ('*What about aluminium? Brass? Plastic? Glass? A paper clip?*') to elicit whether or not a pupil really understood that magnets attract objects with iron in them. If the purpose of the question is to find out whether the pupil understands what magnets do and don't attract, then a focused question may be more effective. It will sometimes be necessary, however, to ask supplementary questions, to ensure that the pupil really does understand, and is not simply repeating a slogan without comprehension.

✳ Transcript

Teacher:	What sort of things do magnets pick up?
Pupil:	Things that have got iron in them.
Teacher:	Can you give me some examples?
Pupil:	A nail, a paper clip.
Teacher:	So if it's only iron that magnets attract, why do those magnetic tin openers pick up the lid of a tin can?
Pupil:	It must have some iron in it.
Teacher:	That's right.

More effective in this context, however, might be questions related to a practical test. Are the pupils operational? Can they actually use their knowledge in some way? This can be an important indicator of their understanding, as well as an extension of it, so I shall return to this same topic below.

Practical tests – knowledge, skill and behaviour

Children may know something, but not be able to apply their knowledge. Teachers often have to check whether their pupils have a particular skill. This can often be done in a natural setting. You can tell whether someone can play a simple melody on a recorder by simply listening carefully when they are attempting to do so. An example of the assessment of knowledge and skill in a natural setting is the way that National Vocational Qualifications (NVQs) are awarded.

The requirements for certification are based on what are called 'Performance Criteria'. The final assessment of them is not determined by a written examination, but is done by an Assessor who assesses them in their workplace, while they are actually doing the job for which they seek a qualification.

If the skill or form of behaviour is not occurring naturally, then the teacher may ask for it to be demonstrated: 'Show me how you brush your teeth'; 'Let me hear you play that line of music'; 'See if you can make this piece of wood a bit smoother'. If the teacher wants to assess how much a pupil knows about magnets and how they work, in other words, to see if they are *operational*, as well as *knowledgeable*, then it is not difficult to set a simple practical test. Assemble a set of ten or twelve objects. These could include a paper clip, a nail, a strip of brass, aluminium, a copper wire, a piece of plastic, a strip of cardboard, a piece of glass or perspex, a pencil lead. Pupils are then asked to put these objects into two piles. The first of these, the 'Yes' pile, should contain the objects they think will be picked up by the magnet. The second, the 'No' pile, those they believe will not be attracted to a magnet. Their decisions will reveal to the teacher what they know, or how much they have learned about magnetism.

A common misconception amongst pupils is that magnets will pick up all metals, when in fact they will attract only the objects with iron in them. This kind of simple diagnostic skills test allows the teacher to ask questions: 'Why did you put the copper in the "Yes" pile?' 'Because it's a metal.' The answers to these questions give important diagnostic insights into what pupils know. The link between assessment and learning is strengthened if the teacher gives pupils a magnet, so they can check their hypotheses, and then ensures that everyone has understood the conclusion that magnets pick up objects with iron in them.

Sometimes teachers need to assess whether or not pupils have acquired a particular skill, like the ability to speak about a certain topic accurately in a foreign language, using relevant vocabulary and with good fluency and intonation. A simple practical test may indicate this quite well. Suppose, for example, the pupils have been studying a foreign language like German, and have covered the topic 'Travel'. The teacher might ask pairs of pupils to devise and then perform a role play, whereby one pupil is looking for a youth hostel and the other plays the proprietor of one that is full, and so must direct the first pupil to

Assessing the child's understanding of 'magnetism'

another hostel that has vacancies.

This would be a useful practical assessment of pupils' linguistic knowledge and skill. It should answer some of the following questions about their competence in this particular aspect of the target language:

- Do they have a grasp of the vocabulary required when asking for or giving directions?
- Is their conversational German grammatically and syntactically accurate?
- What kinds of errors do they make?
- Can they speak German with a reasonable accent, fluency and intonation?

This cluster of linguistic skills, though interlocked, is also separable. For example, if some pupils have a good grasp of vocabulary, reasonable pronunciation, but poor intonation

and little fluency, then they will need special work on the last two, perhaps being encouraged to make a second, more fluent attempt once they have answered a question.

❋ Transcript

Pupil: [Hesitantly, but with accurate pronunciation] Sie … gehen … geradeaus … und dann … nehmen Sie … er … die zweite … Strasse … er … links. [*You go straight on and then you take the second road on the left.*]

Teacher: Noch einmal. [*Again.*] Sie gehen geradeaus und dann nehmen Sie die zweite Strasse links. [Teacher offers a fluent model to the pupil.]

'Are you sure this is a Youth Hostel?'

Pupil: Sie gehen geradeaus und dann nehmen
            Sie die zweite Strasse links. [Spoken
            more fluently and with better
            intonation]
Teacher: Ja, gut. Das war viel besser. [*Yes, good.
            That was much better.*]

Failure to make interim assessments and interventions of this kind in a field like foreign language learning can be disastrous. Once pupils have repeated and rehearsed thousands of mispronunciations, grammatical and syntactical errors, or practised over and over again a form of intonation that reflects their mother tongue rather than the correct patterns of the foreign language they are studying, they will have learned a version of the language that only exists in badly run modern language classrooms. It is a mountainous assignment to arrest, unscramble, and then re-cast a huge amount of learned error, especially in a field like language, where the cumulative effect over days, weeks and months can be colossal. It is much better to assess informally and then amend as necessary on a daily basis.

ACTIVITY 5

Informal assessment of knowledge and skill

Find an opportunity to assess informally a pupil's knowledge and skill in a particular field in which you are engaged. Ask yourself the following:

*   What did you conclude about (a) the pupil's knowledge, (b) the pupil's skill?
*   Were knowledge and skill closely linked – for example, did lack of knowledge affect the degree of skill? Was any lack of skill solely explained by lack of knowledge?

- How did you do the assessment? How valid and reliable do you think it was, given that it was informal? How might you improve such an assessment on a future occasion?

Feedback

What sort of responses do pupils make and what, in turn, do teachers do when pupils answer their questions? An analysis of over 1,000 teachers' questions by Wragg (1993) showed that nearly 60% of them obtained an arguably 'correct' or acceptable response. Of the other replies, about 7% were incorrect, and the rest either attracted a non-verbal reply or no response. About half the teachers' reactions to pupils' replies were in a positive framework, offering approval, assent, or encouragement.

If assessment is to be linked to learning, then feedback, or 'knowledge of results', is an important part of this connection. Absence of feedback may cause uncertainty, as these two extracts from lessons show. In the first, the teacher is trying to find out whether her 6-year-old children understand the difference between hard and soft boiled eggs. She does respond to their answers, but lack of clear feedback about the line of reasoning they are supposed to be following leaves the children confused, and eventually they lose interest.

✳ Transcript

Teacher:	That was the first egg. What is the same about this one?
Pupil 1:	It's smaller.
Teacher:	No, what's the same?
Pupil 1:	Bigger.
Pupil 2:	Shell.
Teacher:	They've got the same shell. What do you mean by the same shell?
Pupil 2:	Same colour.
Pupil 3:	It's outside.
Teacher:	And it's outside?
Pupil 3:	Out of the egg.
Teacher:	'Cos it's a shell it's outside, that's right.
Pupil 4:	A peacock might come out.
Teacher:	Shh! Alex, Alex … Let's see what happens when we open it.… Let's try not to shout, and that means Alex and Royston.

The second extract below reveals a similar uncertainty. The teacher is trying to assess how much the children know and understand about insects. However, he gives no indication that the answers 'spider', 'worm' and 'snail' are incorrect. In the end, lack of feedback helps make the concept become completely indistinct. His attempt at assessment of prior knowledge has itself disrupted comprehension, rather than diagnosed it.

✳ Transcript

Teacher:	I'm going to give you the little word 'insect'. Immediately in your mind there's a picture of something, I expect. There is in mine. What sort of picture have you got, Cassandra?
Pupil 1:	A spider.
Teacher:	OK, you think of a spider. You keep the spider there. Catherine, what about you?
Pupil 2:	[no response]
Teacher:	When I say 'insect' what do you immediately think of – an insect?
Pupil 3:	A ladybird.
Teacher:	Yes, that's right.
Pupil 4:	A worm.
Teacher:	Yes – anything else?
Pupil 3:	A snail.
Teacher:	How do insects move around, Peter?
Pupil 2:	Legs.
Teacher:	How many legs has an insect got?
Pupil 2:	Six.
Teacher:	Yes, six: but do insects get around any other way?
Pupil 2:	Some insects fly.
Teacher:	Yes, some insects use wings. Can you think of an insect that flies?
Pupil 2:	An eagle.
Teacher:	An eagle? Is that an insect? No, it's a bird. A bird is definitely not an insect.

Feedback is especially important in whole class and group assessment as it can affect so many people. If a teacher asks 'What is the capital of France?', many pupils, including those who do not necessarily raise their hand, will hold, suspended in their mind, their 'imagined answer' 'Paris'. If someone's answer is inaudible, or if the teacher does not indicate whether a reply is right or wrong, then all these imagined answers remain unconfirmed. Assessment may well have taken place from the teacher's point of view, but a valuable opportunity to link assessment and learning has been missed.

OBSERVATION AND MONITORING

Doctors, psychologists, social workers, veterinary surgeons, actors, artists, photographers, all these regard observation as an important part of their stock-in-trade. By looking at how people behave, they are able to make an assessment, according to the particular focus of their profession. Teachers also rely on observation, and I have written at greater length elsewhere (Wragg, 1994) about studying individual pupils, events, or interactions in the classroom. There are few certainties and many ambiguities in classroom life, but that does not mean that it is pointless trying to study what is happening. Even careful and considered observation may deceive. The pupil who appears to be concentrating may be day-dreaming, while the one who seems detached may be engrossed. Nevertheless, a great deal can be learned, despite the caution that must be exercised when reaching conclusions.

Assessing priorities is one prime example of the use of observation. The American researcher Jacob Kounin (1970) described the classroom management of teachers who are able to split their attention between the children they are with and the rest of the class, a skill he called 'withitness'. It allows them to decide which children may need help, who appears to have lost interest, which pupils have finished their work, and to respond to those with hands raised, seeking the teacher's attention.

Little time may available, in a busy lesson, for these classroom sweeps, but they are valuable. So too is any time the teacher can find for studying pupils as individuals. How much time and with what degree of interest are they pursuing their task? What use do they make of resources? Do individual members of groups work harmoniously or are they discordant? This is where judicious monitoring becomes a very important part of successful informal assessment and learning.

Most teachers take the trouble to talk to individuals or groups when they walk round the class monitoring a science experiment, coaching a sports group, discussing a technology project, or checking any of the normal written and practical tasks undertaken in school. A few patrol the room, but do not actually scrutinise pupils' work, creating a draught rather than monitoring. Some remain detached in a nearby prep room, stock cupboard, or seated at their desk. Although distractions and competing priorities may be inescapable when teachers are beset by numerous demands, failure to monitor work can lead to disappointment. Occasionally teachers will say that they are surprised at how little work some pupils managed to achieve in a certain period of time, but, had they monitored the work regularly during the lesson, action could have been taken in good time.

When working on their own or in a group, pupils fail to make progress for different reasons. These may include lack of motivation, interference from others, reaching a plateau (or an abyss) where they no longer understand the subject matter, reading or comprehension difficulties, lack of clarity about the purpose and process in which they are engaged, frustration, and several others. Monitoring is a central means of linking informal assessment and learning, precisely because it allows the teacher to identify what is happening and what is needed at the very moment when help may be effective.

Monitoring is not a random occurrence, even though it may often be spontaneous. The mini-interview or conversation between teacher and pupil is an important act of assessment. What is more, it can be bespoke, tailor-made to the individual, not generalised and omni-purpose. 'Explain to me what you've been doing' is a good example of both assessment and learning. The teacher finds out what the pupils know, can do, or misunderstand, while the pupils have to clarify for the teacher, and thus for themselves, what they are learning.

Monitoring of this kind can be particularly important in practical lessons, when pupils are carrying out science experiments, or working on a technology project. There can also be valuable formative assessment in the creative and expressive arts. Assessment in the field of creative endeavour is often seen as controversial. Teachers are particularly sensitive about the dangers of undermining children's confidence when they make their first hesitant brush strokes, attempt a rudimentary piece of musical composition, write a poem or story, or take their early steps in dance. Yet pupils often crave an evaluation of what they are doing, and there are numerous ways of giving it without demolishing their enthusiasm.

What is crucial is the language of discourse. A group of pupils is sitting on a grassy bank, making sketches of the scene before them, so that they can return to class and compose a drawing or painting. The teacher is moving from child to child, looking over their shoulder at what they have done so far in their partially completed drawings. His assessment of some children's work is that there is no evidence of light and shade. Amongst the many language choices available to him for this important formative assessment, ranging from the ham-fisted to the non-committal, are the six below.

'That won't do. Just look at it. There's no depth. It's absolutely flat.'

'Look more carefully at what you're drawing. You're not really looking properly.'

'Where is the light coming from? ... That's right, it's high on the right. So look at that tree. Can you see how the right-hand side is shining and the other side is darker? See if you can get that contrast into your picture by using a bit of shading down the left side.'

'You need to use more light and shade in your picture. Let me show you what I mean. Have a look at this sketch I've just done of that same tree.'

'What are you trying to achieve here? Can you see any way of making it closer to what you're trying to do?'

'Yes fine. That's just fine. Carry on.'

 ACTIVITY 6

Assessing creative work

Look at the pupil's drawing of a scene with a tree in it. Consider possible teacher responses, including the following:

1 Look at each of the six teacher responses above and decide (a) what seems to be the intention behind them, and (b) what might be the reaction from different types of pupil to each one.
2 What would you say to the pupil yourself about the drawing, and what would be the purpose of what you would like to see happening?
3 Think of a situation in another creative field, or activity where imagination and invention were central features – music, story/poetry writing, dance, drama – and consider what

formative evaluation you would want to give during the process.
4 Look at your own practice in lessons where creative imagination might have a place. How do you actually respond to pupils' work, and do you feel you need to modify your approach in the light of reflection?

FAIR OPPORTUNITIES

Whereas in many formal assessments pupils sit down for a lengthy period of time and, in theory at any rate, all have the same opportunity to show what they can do, informal assessment can be more sporadic and *ad hoc*, with some pupils getting much more attention than others. There are several pitfalls for the unwary. For example, some classroom research (Wragg, 1994) has shown that during whole-class teaching, many of the questions tend to be directed towards those pupils sitting in a V-shaped arc in front of the teacher. Fewer are addressed to pupils at the back or down the sides of the room.

Pupils who want to be involved in classroom interaction often choose the 'busy' central seats, while quieter ones may opt for a place where there is less chance of being called. Thus teachers may obtain a false picture of a class's knowledge or competence if they base their assessment solely on the contributions of those most eager to offer them. Distributing questions widely and calling on pupils who have not necessarily raised their hands, can help spread evaluative questioning more equitably.

Similarly it is easy, during monitoring, to concentrate on the badly behaved, the most demanding, the pupils nearest the front and centre of the room, and neglect those who are more quiet and reflective. It is also possible, often without realising it, to ignore children who seem on the surface to be managing their task, but who might, on closer inspection, be lost within it. Some children are more reluctant to ask for help than others. Fairly distributed and judicious monitoring allows all children the chance to benefit from the teacher's help.

This does not rule out the possibility that one pupil's need for assistance might, at certain times, exceed that of another. The concept of 'fairness' does not require exactly equal amounts of time from the teacher for every single child, but rather a considered appraisal of who would benefit from informal assessment on different occasions and in various contexts. A pupil who is struggling with a task or concept today might, after a teacher's intervention, be confidently surging ahead with it tomorrow and need less immediate help.

Unit 4

FORMAL METHODS OF ASSESSMENT

Understanding the many formal methods of assessing children's knowledge, skills, or qualities requires more than just the possession of a bag of tricks. There are plenty of 'techniques' available, but it is important to know what they offer and, when there is a choice, which kind of formal assessment makes best sense in what circumstances. This means understanding how tests are constructed, what they are attempting to assess, and how they are scored, interpreted and used. Many of the most commonly used tests are norm-referenced, that is, they place a pupil on some kind of scale in relationship to all the other possible candidates, as was described in Unit 2. Increasingly, however, different types of test are being used, based on different assumptions and procedures.

As will be discussed further in Unit 6, there is sometimes confusion when people treat one kind of test as if it is another. For example, in a standardised norm-referenced test, the time available is usually limited. If, during the standardisation procedures, pupils had been allowed exactly one hour, and not a minute more, then all the 'norms' and standardised scores would be thrown into disarray, were candidates to be allowed an extra ten minutes.

In certain kinds of criterion-referenced test, however, the question is whether or not pupils know or can do certain things. They may, therefore, need a little longer to display their knowledge and competence. The driving test is designed to find out whether or not people are fit to be let loose on the road, not whether they can perform certain operations in exactly 30 minutes. If a candidate is slowed up by heavy traffic, then it would be natural to allow a little extra time, rather than click a stopwatch and withhold the chance to reverse and perform an emergency stop. Teachers would be too limited if they only knew and used one kind of test, or confused the intentions and procedures of one form of assessment with those of another.

Formal assessment is not just a matter of constructing and administering written tests containing several discrete items. Essays, performances, creative achievements, practical skills and many other types of human proficiency may at one time or another be part of a formal assessment. These many kinds of 'evidence' can all be considered and it is important that they are assessed fairly, especially if they are to have some influence on what pupils have learned in the past and may learn in the future.

TEST CONSTRUCTION

There has been considerable refinement in the construction of tests over the years. Researchers using one of the well-tried tests of reading, which gives, say, an average score of 100, with two-thirds of candidates spread between the scores 85 and 115, will find that, if they test a sizeable sample of pupils, they too obtain this kind of distribution. That is not to say the test is perfect, but that it has been carefully standardised. Tests that are used on a wide scale have usually been put through a set of procedures similar to the following. It is worth looking at these closely, because teachers may well want to go through a much simplified version of events when constructing their own tests.

Step 1: Define the content

If the test is to be valid, then it must measure what it is supposed to measure. This means defining as carefully as possible the area being assessed. Is the intention to measure a characteristic which may affect learning, like verbal intelligence, or a personality trait like 'determination'? Or is it to measure achievement in a particular field of study? If so, what subject is involved? Is the test to assess knowledge of key facts and concepts, attitudes, skills, or a mixture of these? Is the area regarded as a single topic, or are there certain sub-topics which should be tested? For example, is a mathematics test only going to assess how well children can handle 'number', or will it also address 'algebra', 'probability', 'geometry', 'measures'?

If there are sub-topics, are these all equally important, or should the various mini-themes be weighted in some way? Should a maths test assign half its marks for 'number', a quarter for 'geometry', and a quarter for 'probability and statistics'? Ought there to be a single mark or grade, or would it be better to have a profile of scores, reflecting the various sub-topics? These decisions ought to reflect the balance of what is being taught, or what is regarded as most and least important in the situation in which the assessment takes place. Test constructors may consult textbooks, interview teachers, observe lessons, talk to subject experts, but they should make the effort to define the field and the focus.

Step 2: Assemble a set of items

There are many types of item that may feature in a test, so it is common practice to collect far more possibilities than can actually be used. These are then tried out on a sample of people typical of those likely to take the finished test. This should help identify potential snags, such as ambiguous or unclear wording. Suppose an item is intended to test whether pupils can calculate the area of two differently shaped rectangles, a tall thin one and a short fat one. The first draft of the question asks: 'Is A bigger than B?' Trials may reveal that some pupils interpret 'bigger than' as referring solely to the height, so they consider only how tall the rectangle is. If the intention of the test is to see whether pupils can calculate the area of a rectangle, then a second trial would probably

change the wording to 'Which rectangle has the greater area, A or B? Show how you worked out your answer'.

With criterion-referenced tests the items are often in the 'can do' category, specially chosen to link closely to whatever criteria are laid down in the syllabus or area of study being assessed. The criteria to be met are then usually phrased in terms of what pupils should know or be able to do, like 'multiply two three-digit numbers', 'perform a handstand unaided', or 'be able to recognise and name the letters of the alphabet'. Items would then be assembled in clusters to reflect these objectives:

$425 \times 235 = ?$
$328 \times 549 = ?$

or an instruction to the tester:

Point to each of these letters and ask the pupil, 'What letter is this…?'
B D G A T Y E C

Once a pool of potential items has been assembled, the test can be constructed using a range of these, often starting with simpler questions and working up to the more difficult ones. So the next step works out what is easy and what is hard for pupils.

Step 3: Analyse the items

There are many ways of analysing trial items, one of which, checking for ambiguities or poor wording, has already been mentioned. When constructing a test with several items in it, however, the tester usually needs to know how difficult each item was. One simple index is to see what percentage of the sample got each question right. An item that 22% got right is then, in theory at any rate, 'harder' than one that 66% answered correctly.

However, this is only one part of the story. The test constructor also needs to know whether the item really does discriminate between pupils of different attainment levels. The techniques for doing this vary according to whether norm-referenced or criterion-referenced tests are being developed.

Norm-referenced tests

The technique commonly used to discover how well a test differentiates is to develop for each item what is called a *discrimination index*. The procedure for doing this is to look at the total test scores of the group that has taken the trial version of the test. Often the top scoring quarter of candidates is then compared with the bottom scoring quarter.

Let us assume that 200 pupils take a test. There will thus be 50 high-scoring and 50 low-scoring pupils in the top and bottom quarters. Let us suppose that on Item A of the test 45 pupils in the high-scoring group got the correct answer, but only 15 in the bottom quarter gave the right response. One simple discrimination index, when there are equal numbers in the top and bottom samples, is calculated as follows:

How many 'top quarter' pupils got the right answer?	45
How many 'bottom quarter' pupils got the right answer?	15
Take the bottom quarter figure from the top quarter figure.	$45 - 15 = 30$
Divide the answer by the total number of pupils in the top quarter.	$30 \div 50 = 0.6$

The *discrimination index*, therefore, would be +0.6. The *higher* this figure is, the better the item is said to discriminate. If all 50 high-performing pupils got the right answer and not one of the lower performing children did so, then the discrimination index would be: $50 - 0 = 50$, which, divided by the total number of pupils in the 'top' group (50) would give the absolute maximum score of +1.

Imagine the exact opposite, an item which every member of the 'bottom' group got right, but all the 'top' group got wrong! The discrimination index would then be $0 - 50 = -50$, which, divided by the total number of pupils in the 'top' group (50) would give the absolute minimum score of −1.

Any positive score, therefore, means the top group did better than the bottom group on that particular item, while any item with a negative score would mean the bottom group did better than the top group. Usually items with a higher *positive* discrimination index would be used in tests, but it is common to have certain 'easy' items at the beginning of a test to help children warm up and feel confident, so the discrimination index of these items may be lower if most pupils tend to get them right.

Indeed, if every item used had a discrimination index of +0.9 or above, then the complete test would not be a sufficiently good discriminator across the whole range of achievement, as most pupils would be getting every item wrong, and a small number would be answering most items correctly. In practice, norm-referenced tests are designed to scale people from top to bottom on the usual bell-shaped curve, with about two-thirds of candidates near the middle and fewer at the extremes.

Criterion-referenced tests

Since the aim of the criterion-referenced test is not to spread candidates across a normal distribution curve, but rather to discover who can do what, the approach to item analysis is different. In some cases 'face validity' applies, as described in Unit 2. For example, in the field of physical education, a formal assessment of children's performance at the age of 11 may include the statement 'Can swim 25 metres, unaided and safely'. The only feasible way of assessing who can do this is to let children try to swim from one end of a 25-metre pool to the other, under safe conditions. There is no point in getting them to write an essay about it instead.

In a criterion-referenced test it is common to have several similar items in a cluster for each of the stated criteria. If someone wanted to know whether children can add two two-digit numbers, in other words 'do tens and units', then several items may be used:

A	B	C	D	E
12+	23+	46+	88+	59+
12	11	53	11	30
—	—	—	—	—

It is then possible to see which pupils got which answers right. Supposing five pupils completed the five questions above. The following table might be drawn up, where 1 indicates a correct answer to the sum, and 0 means an incorrect answer.

	A	B	C	D	E	TOTAL
Ann	1	1	1	1	1	5
Brian	1	1	0	0	0	2
Carina	1	1	0	1	0	3
David	1	1	0	1	1	4
Elaine	1	0	0	0	0	1
TOTAL	5	4	1	3	2	

This gives useful information about the test items. First of all we can see that Ann and David have the best grasp of tens and units, since they obtained 5 and 4 correct answers respectively,

Criterion-referenced test in physical education – can the child throw and catch a ball?

while Brian and Elaine come lowest with 2 and 1 correct responses. We can also deduce that item A, 12 + 12, was the easiest item, as all five children got it right, whereas item C, 46 + 53, was the hardest, only Ann, the highest scoring pupil, giving a correct reply.

What happens next depends on the purposes and intentions of the tester. If someone wanted to *scale the items in order of difficulty,* then the results suggest the best order for putting the simplest questions first and the hardest last would be A–B–D–E–C. Should the intention be to provide a *diagnostic profile,* then any pupil unable to complete a sum as easy as item A, 12 + 12, would appear to have no functional grasp of tens and units. Pupils like Brian, Carina and Elaine may not be able to handle a zero, as they all got item E wrong, 59 + 30, though one would need to inspect their answer and talk to them to see whether this

was a right conclusion. Ann and David should be ready to progress to higher level work, though it would be interesting to see why David went wrong on item C, 46 + 53.

In a large-scale criterion-referenced test, where hundreds or thousands of children are involved, the tester would have to decide how many items have to be correctly answered for a pupil to qualify for the criterion 'can add two two-digit numbers'. Usually this has to be a majority of possible items, but it depends how rigorously the criterion is to be applied. A strict rule would be that all the items have to be answered correctly, but it would be more common to require six, seven, or eight out of ten. The analysis of the items similar to that for norm-referenced tests would indicate which ones had been correctly answered by those like Ann, Carina and David, who could handle most of the questions.

The Rasch model

There are other possibilities than those described above. One which has been used widely in national testing is the Rasch model. It is too complex to describe fully, but a longer analysis has been given by Satterly (1981). It is mentioned here to show that there are numerous ways of compiling and using test items. The two main factors in the Rasch approach are: (1) the pupil's ability, and (2) the item's level of difficulty.

The test constructor assembles a list of items. These are then given to a large sample of pupils. From the results it is possible to see what proportion of children got each item right, irrespective of age. Most 15-year-olds might get it right, but hardly any 7-year-olds. Once the level of difficulty of an item is known, it can be put into an 'item bank' with its 'difficulty label' attached. When tests are compiled, so that assessors can measure standards of achievement over time, items can thus be drawn out from the bank. The Rasch model has been controversial, since children may get a sample question wrong not solely because they are of low ability, but because their teacher has not actually covered the topic. Thus the 'difficulty label' may reflect fashions, or curriculum content, rather than indicate the true intellectual toughness of the concept or question.

Step 4: Construct the final version of the test

Once individual items have been checked out under Step 3, it remains to decide which, of what might be a large pool of possibilities, should be included in the final version of the test. The issue of *length* needs to be considered, so a sample of children of different ages and abilities might be assembled to see how much they could complete in 15, 30 or more minutes. The weighting of the various elements of the test will also determine the construction of the test. In a maths test, if 'number' is to be more heavily weighted than 'geometry' or 'probability', it may need more items, or the items may have to be more demanding, though this is not always essential.

It is customary to *phase* tests according to the difficulty of items, so that 'easier' items come earlier in the test, and in norm-referenced tests there are usually a number of more demanding items later on, so that the whole ability range can be tested. In criterion-referenced tests, clusters of easier and harder questions might be directly linked to lower and higher grade levels of the

award. There may also be 'gateways', that is, rules that you cannot move on to try the higher grade unless you have satisfied the criteria for the lower grade first.

This can sometimes be unfair. For example, in one maths test for 7-year-olds, the grade levels progressed as follows:

Level 1   simple sums
Level 2   questions about throwing dice
Level 3   questions about spending pocket money

There were examples of children who could have handled the questions on pocket money, but who were barred from taking them as they had not been familiar with dots being equivalent to numbers in the throwing of dice.

In some public examinations for older pupils there are different 'tiers', and this can also be unfair. Pupils and their teachers have to decide in advance whether to take a 'basic' or a 'higher' set of papers. For example, in one examination the 'Foundation level' covers grades C to G. No matter how brilliantly pupils perform, they cannot get a grade A or B. The 'Higher' level covers grades A to D and candidates who just fail to reach the required standard for grade D cannot be given a grade E, F, or G. This may mean that, for some pupils, the grade they get does not reflect their true ability, but is rather a reflection of the decision they or their teacher made about which tier of examination to enter.

Another consideration is the *level of interest* of the test. If candidates are bored by the tedium of the assessment, then they may not do themselves justice. Test constructors often try to vary the activities, so that different types of response are required, like closed answers to some parts, but discursive answers and essay-type responses in other sections.

a ACTIVITY 7

Constructing a test

Shortage of time often means that teachers are pressed into devising their own tests intuitively, with little opportunity to evaluate them systematically. It is worth spending a bit more time on constructing a particular test from time to time, as a great deal can be learned that will be of future value.

1   Choose a topic which is suitable and for

which the time is right to give a formal test.

2 Decide the central purposes of the test and then map out the major knowledge, skills, concepts, etc., that might be tested.

3 Draw up some test items, in each case, that would be suitable for testing the particular knowledge, skill, concept, or whatever, deciding which type of item would be best.

4 Try to work out the best running order for them.

5 Administer the test and score it.

6 Analyse the items individually as described in this unit.

7 Discuss the test with some of the pupils and see how the test appears to reflect what they have learned, and also what they learned from taking the test.

8 Recast the test, as necessary, in the light of what you have learned, and try to give it again on a future occasion to a similar group of pupils.

TYPES OF FORMAL ASSESSMENT

A wide range of possibilities may be used in formal assessment. The reasons for using each of them may vary, and they are not always related directly to pupils' learning. For example, ease of administration may well be a factor. A cluster of short items may sometimes be preferred largely because they can be scored easily. These are sometimes called 'objective' tests, as they often require no more than the ticking of a true/false box, or the selection of one answer from a list of possibilities, and in the scoring they may even be untouched by human hand. Indeed, many of the commercially produced tests of this kind are designed to be scored by a machine which simply identifies a tick or a filled-in box, rather like a lottery ticket machine.

Some subject areas lend themselves more easily to segmentation than others. If there are discrete facts or concepts that can stand alone, then it is not difficult to assemble these into sets of separate items and test each of them.

Insects have six legs	True ☐	False ☐
Insects have five parts to their body	True ☐	False ☐
The middle part of an insect is called the	Thorax ☐	Abdomen ☐

It is harder, though not impossible, to disentangle more complex fields into separate items.

'Paintings are usually attractive – true or false?' would leave the poor candidate asking too many questions about the meaning and context of the question.

Multiple choice

There are many kinds of multiple choice item. A common form is a question with four possible answers. Only one of these is correct and the other three act as 'distractors', that is, valid-looking alternatives which those who do not know the field sufficiently, or who are merely guessing, may select. In the following multiple choice item, B is the right answer, while the other three act as distractors.

Britain declared war on Germany in 1939 because:
A The Archduke of Austria was assassinated by a German
B Hitler occupied Poland and refused to withdraw
C U-boats had been sinking British passenger ships
D German planes bombed London

The 'correct' answer must be unambiguously right and the distractors need to be credible-looking alternatives, though clearly wrong. If the distractors are too obvious, then the item will not really test children's knowledge, but rather their intelligence.

Other forms of multiple choice item include:

Sentence completion	The chemical formula for water is … (a) HO_2 (b) H_2O
Insertion	Fill the gap, using one of the alternatives: 'A … is an animal which suckles its young' (a) mammal (b) reptile
Multiple response	Tick any of the following statements which are correct … (followed by a list with more than one acceptable answer)

If every question has four possible answers, then pupils could obtain 25% purely by guessing, as chance would yield a quarter of correct responses. There are various ways of dealing with this. One is to adjust the score. For example, if there are 20 questions and a candidate has 14 correct and 6 incorrect answers, then the raw score would be 14, or 70%. The adjusted score would need to eliminate the chance or 'guessing' element, by making a score of 25% the equivalent of zero, as anyone could obtain it by sticking in a pin each time. An adjusted score might, therefore, be calculated as follows:

$$14 \text{ (correct answers)} - \frac{6 \text{ (incorrect answers)}}{3 \text{ (number of distractors)}}$$
$$= 12$$

The corrected score, therefore, would be 12, or 60%. If you try substituting various possible scores in the formula above, you will see how it compensates for guesswork. A pin sticker with 5 correct answers would have an adjusted score of zero, while a candidate with 17 correct answers would show an adjusted score of 16, or 80%.

Another way of penalising those who merely guess is to weight some of the distractors more heavily, for example to deduct two or more marks if anyone actually ticks them. If a question asked 'The dates of the Second World War are ...?' with the correct answer '1939 to 1945', then the distractor '1938 to 1944' might incur no further penalty beyond the single lost mark, while a distractor like '1559 to 1672' might be given a weighted penalty, as it is so far out it would only be ticked by candidates who were guessing.

Diagnostic tests

There are many uses for diagnostic tests, although the medical associations of the portmanteau word 'diagnosis', as was described in Unit 2, ought not to label perfectly normal people as being in some way 'defective'. Among the common purposes are:

(a) to measure progress over time under various headings and subheadings;
(b) to identify areas where the pupil seems to have understood, and those where particular forms of knowledge, skill or understanding have not yet been mastered;
(c) to analyse errors (in the case of reading tests sometimes referred to as 'miscues');
(d) to assess readiness to progress to more demanding work.

Diagnostic tests can be either norm-referenced or criterion-referenced. The norm-referenced ones tend to place pupils on sub-tests relative to their age group. Thus an 8-year-old child doing a maths test might be seen to be achieving as follows:

Number 9.5 years   *Shape and space* 7.2 years
Measures 8.0 years

This would mean the pupil is above average, performing like a 9-year-old in 'number', below average in 'shape and space', with the achievement level of a 7-year-old, but average in 'measures', where the score is such as would be predicted for the pupil's chronological age of 8.

Other diagnostic tests take a criterion-referenced approach, so that the teacher, and indeed the pupil, can look at and act on the individual item scores, rather than on a total mark. Whether someone obtained 32% or 76%, or performed like or unlike others of the same age, is not the principal focus of this kind of diagnostic test, interesting and illuminating though that sort of information may be. The major purpose of criterion-referenced diagnostic tests is to construct a profile highlighting which particular aspects of the subject or topic have been grasped and which are not yet understood, if necessary right down to the individual test item level. A 'mastery' (for want of a better word) profile of this kind might look more like this, in abbreviated form:

Number   Place value up to 1000 ✓
     Subtract two two-digit numbers ✗
     Add two two-digit numbers ✓
     5 times multiplication table ✓
Shape and space   Classify two-dimensional shapes ✓
     Classify three-dimensional shapes ✗
Measures   Use non-standard units (strides) ✓
     Use standard units (metres) ✗

One common criticism of diagnostic tests is that they may concentrate too much on 'weaknesses', and that they may focus too much on what is easily coded under particular headings, so that the total picture is lost amid a mass of labels. Another point often made is that many of the sub-tests can overlap, rather than be completely separate. On a reading test, for example, 'letter identification', 'word recognition', 'spelling', 'comprehension' may be interdependent, rather than disconnected.

Sensitive use of diagnostic tests, however, can be informative for both pupils and teachers. If they are not used crudely and if teachers are aware of the dangers of giving pupils too much of a sense of failure and no sense of success, then they can help learning by showing where effort needs to be placed. Not all subject matter lends itself easily to the diagnostic approach, as some aspects of human activity are more diffuse in nature. On the other hand, in fields like art, which are sometimes regarded as less open to analysis and systematic teaching, pupils do need to be able to hold a pencil or brush properly, appreciate the importance of composition, know how to mix and apply paint, to handle and shape clay, and numerous other aspects of the subject.

Essays

Single test items are often appropriate when discrete pieces of knowledge or specific skills are being assessed. When more complex knowledge is being evaluated, then essays are frequently employed. However, the essay is notorious for sometimes producing great disparities between different markers, and is often regarded as a less reliable form of assessment for this reason. Yet careful thought can make essay-type questions more reliable and very useful, both for pupils, who may well learn by having to give thought and shape to what they have been studying, and for teachers, who can see what understanding or misconceptions have been acquired.

Various terms may be used to describe different sorts of essay question, like 'restricted' and 'extended', or 'focused' and 'open'. A *restricted* or

'When I asked you to explain "Supply and Demand" to a Martian, I didn't mean it literally'

focused essay tries to ensure that the respondent addresses a particular issue or set of issues and is not able to range too widely. It will involve titles such as 'Describe two examples of animals adapting to their environment', or 'Analyse the likely effects of mortgage restrictions on the housing market'. An *extended* or more *open* essay title in the same two fields would allow pupils the chance to reveal a wider range of knowledge, so it is likely to pose questions such as: 'Discuss the effects that the environment can have on the lives of animals', or 'Explain to an intelligent Martian how the law of supply and demand works in our economy'.

Essays allow different kinds of knowledge and skill to be displayed. Pupils may well be able to demonstrate the following: describing, analysing, comparing and contrasting, making inferences, generalising from information available, classifying and grouping, synthesising information from different sources, evaluating, applying principles to situations and problems, imagining and speculating, reaching valid conclusions. Well-phrased essay titles require careful choice of words, so that pupils are clear what is supposed to be the nature and principal thrust of their response.

Properly conceived marking schemes can help reduce the unreliability of essay questions. The assessors need to be clear what they are looking for. If the candidate is supposed to be able to generate, organise and express clearly a set of ideas, or present arguments for and against a proposition with supporting evidence, then this can be stated in advance so that both pupil and marker are clear about the purpose of the essay question in a particular examination. Otherwise subjectivity is at a premium and different markers may show considerable divergence from each other.

 ACTIVITY 8

Double marking an essay

Take a set of ten essays, not necessarily written by pupils you teach. Read them through and give each one a mark out of twenty.

Get a fellow teacher or student to act as an independent second marker, but neither of you should write on the essays or give any indication of your own marks.

Compare the two sets of marks. Discuss similarities and differences. Are there any essays about which you appear to disagree more markedly? If so, why is this?

Mark another set of ten essays, but this time agreeing in advance with your fellow marker what sort of criteria you will apply. Are there more or fewer differences between you?

Ask the pupils to assess their own essays. Compare the teachers' perceptions with theirs.

Practical and oral tests

There are many situations where a practical and/or oral test makes more sense than some kind of written assessment on its own. Most citizens would feel more secure on the roads knowing that motorists had had to pass a practical test, not just sit a theory paper. In numerous fields, such as art, cookery, design, foreign languages, music, science, sports coaching and performance, technology, vocational education, it makes sense to assess practical skills as well as underpinning knowledge. As in other forms, students themselves can learn from the assessment of their practical competence if it is carried out intelligently and if they receive feedback.

Some of the same issues as were mentioned about essay questions apply to practical and oral examinations as well. It could be a highly subjective business if no forethought were given to the purpose, form and evaluation of practical and oral competence. Those who are well groomed and articulate, but not necessarily knowledgeable and competent, might make a disproportionately favourable impression, just as the glib and fluent writer might score an unfairly high mark with an unprepared essay reader.

The assessment of vocational qualifications may be based almost entirely on practical and oral assessment. The National Vocational Qualifications (NVQs), which are offered at five levels ranging form beginner to degree level, have an extremely complex structure and language. First of all the programmes have been divided up into a number of *units*, which may be *mandatory* (you must do them) or *optional* (you choose to do them). Each unit consists of *elements*. Each element contains *performance criteria* (things you are supposed to be able to do), *range statements* (the context in which you are expected to achieve the standard), *underpinning knowledge/ understanding* (what you need to know and understand). There are no formal 'sit-down' written examinations, as the emphasis is on practical abilities.

- Candidates receive a *pass* for each unit successfully completed. There are no grades. In the event of not passing, the unit can be taken again, as often as necessary.
- To be successful they must satisfy an assessor that they can do the jobs or tasks which have been specified in each element of the unit.
- Assessments are usually carried out by locally trained people. They are often the same people who have been teaching the candidates during the weeks or months leading up to the formal assessment.
- Assessments are meant to happen in a real work place while candidates are doing the actual job. Since it is not always possible to examine people in their work place, many colleges have created 'realistic work environments', such as restaurants, reception areas, nurseries and hairdressing salons, where assessment can also take place.
- Candidates must satisfy the assessment requirements by keeping a personal *portfolio of evidence* and/or by *demonstrating competences* while the assessor is observing normal work routines.

There has been a great deal of criticism of NVQs, partly because of the opaque language involved and partly because of what is seen as a mechanical approach to the assessment of practical work. There is no need, however, for practical and oral competence to be assessed in either a slipshod or an over-bureaucratic way. It is perfectly possible to work out a set of criteria for assessment, fair and manageable procedures, possibly involving a tape or video record, or a second assessor, that will not only give an appraisal of someone's competence, but also offer information back to them that may help improve their practical and oral competence.

Interpreting scores

When tests have been administered, they are marked according to the instructions. Often this will produce a set of marks that indicate what the pupils has achieved. In the case of criterion-referenced tests this may be a 'profile' or a set

Assessing vocational skills
Reproduced courtesy of Exeter College

of 'levels'. With many commercially produced norm-referenced tests, teachers may have to convert the *raw score* to a *standardised score*, using the table of norms provided. This usually involves looking up each pupil's age and converting the score accordingly.

For example, let us assume that a class takes a test where the standardised score for the average pupil will be 100, and most children will range between 80 and 120. Take the case of someone who has obtained a raw score of 35. The table may show that, in the case of a child aged between 7 years nine months and 8 years two months, this would convert to a standardised score of 87, putting the child on the 19th percentile, that is towards the bottom compared with others of the same age. However, if a child aged between 5 years nine months and 6 years two months obtained 35 on the same test, then the table might yield a standardised score of 104, the 61st percentile for that age group, and an above average performance. Test scores and their conversions must always be done carefully, as small arithmetical errors can sometimes cause big differences.

PUBLIC EXAMINATIONS

These occupy only a tiny percentage of the total time spent on assessment in schools, yet they often provide the basic data on which a pupil, a teacher, a school, a whole area even, or indeed the nation itself, may be judged. Public examinations are designed for many purposes, some of which will be discussed in more detail in Unit 6. Various interest groups may expect them to provide, among other outcomes, evidence of teachers' effectiveness, pupils' learning, national or local improvement from one year to the next, comparative performance between one school or local authority and another, predictions of future potential and performance, criteria for selection of the most able or suited, identification of those who need help, and motivation for pupils to achieve their best and focus their efforts.

It would be difficult for any form of assessment, let alone a national test taken by millions, to meet all these aspirations. A good diagnostic test is not necessarily a good measure of comparative standards or year-on-year progress, and vice versa. Nonetheless, public examinations are partly intended to inform the citizenry about progress in the education system for which it has paid its taxes, so the accountability angle cannot be ignored.

With millions of pounds of funding behind it, public examining has become a major industry. Test agencies and examination boards are able to develop a wide range of types of assessment. Most of the forms of assessment described in this book have been used at one time or another as part of the public examination process. That includes informal and continuous assessment alongside formal test papers taken under strict conditions of security for fixed periods of time in a room patrolled by supervising teachers.

It is this last form of assessment that can cause pupils the greatest difficulty, especially the first few times they experience it. Even older students taking university examinations can still feel the pressures and not achieve their best, or may commit one of the common errors under formal time-constrained conditions, like not sharing out the time available across all the questions. That is why it is worth giving pupils some experience of formal examination conditions before they ever take the official public version.

'Exam technique' is often discussed as if it is some mysterious separate talent. If pupils have learned nothing, then the finest techniques in the world will be useless. It is better to think in terms of the elementary tactical errors that the inexperienced or those under pressure may make. They include the following:

1 *Not sharing out the time properly*   Practising timed answers and working out how much time is available for each question is one step pupils may take.
2 *Not reading the instructions carefully*   When asked to answer *either* question 3a *or* question 3b, some will do both.
3 *Failing to make a start*   Since classroom and homework assignments are often open-ended in terms of time available, having to make an immediate start can seem unusual.
4 *Not reading the question carefully*   Failing to follow the instructions to 'Compare and contrast …', 'Analyse …', 'Solve …', 'Describe …', 'Discuss …', 'Show how …'.
5 *Not answering the question set*   Many candidates, unused to focusing their argument inside a few minutes, may drift off the point, or answer the question they wish had been set, rather than the one that is actually set.
6 *Leaving gaps*   Pupils often fail to understand how a formal examination marking scheme works, and do not realise that they can gain marks for partially correct answers, so they simply leave a whole question or section blank. Explaining the marking criteria and conventions to them may avoid this.
7 *Poor spelling, grammar and punctuation*   Some examiners are instructed to deduct marks in all subjects for poor English.
8 *Not leaving time to check*   Inexperienced candidates may either mistime their responses and find no time left at the end to review their script, or may finish early but not bother to look through their paper.

Given the small amount of difference between various grades in some public exams, these elementary errors may lead to an underestimate of pupils' abilities and achievements.

ASSESSMENT IN ACTION

Whether or not assessment leads to pupil learning depends very much on how it is actually carried out in schools and classrooms. What are in theory identical procedures can work out quite differently in practice. Pupils' age and background, the subjects being taught, the beliefs and favoured practices of the teacher, the varying purposes and uses of assessment, and the constraints of time, space, or resources, can all exert a significant influence on what takes place.

The age of the class alone can be a significant determinant of policy and practice. What is desirable or feasible with 5-year-olds may be quite different from preferred practice with 15-year-olds. Although young pupils can begin to take responsibility for making judgements about their own progress, with older pupils this should have become a matter of routine for, once they enter adult life, many will have to evaluate and monitor their own achievements on a daily basis. In this unit we shall consider assessment in various subjects and settings, including those where practical work is being assessed, and the important matter of self-assessment, which empowers pupils to evaluate their own work.

SUBJECT ASSESSMENT

It is not feasible to cover every single school subject and cross-curricular theme in a book of this kind, so it will only be possible to consider briefly one or two issues in a number of subjects, in order to illustrate what is shared and what is unique in various contexts.

Expressive arts

There has often been resistance to the assessment of children's work in arts lessons, partly because some teachers were anxious to distance the subject from other domains that put a high premium on assessment, and partly because it was thought to be a more subjective process, and therefore more difficult. The shift towards greater use of criterion-referenced assessment has led to some assessments in art, for example, involving both formative and summative evaluation, with a focus on the actual *process* of creating a work of art, as well as on the final version of it.

A profile approach to art assessment, covering both process and outcome, might involve such features as the following, when appropriate. Not all aspects would necessarily be assessed, nor would they all be equally weighted.

- Developing ideas from observation
- Gathering resources and materials that stimulate ideas
- Exploring various two- and three-dimensional media to decide on the most suitable form of expression
- Reviewing and modifying work as it progresses
- The quality of the finished work of art
- The ability to evaluate and improve what has been created

In the field of *music,* by contrast, public examinations for instrumental performance and singing have been well established for many years, so both pupils and teachers are much more used to graded examinations, for which pupils study and play set pieces and demonstrate practical skill, or knowledge of music theory. In music, as in other arts subjects, the debate often centres on whether assessment should involve a holistic approach, which involves the evaluator giving an overall impressionistic mark, or whether some kind of criteria should be drawn up, involving separate but related aspects of the piece being played or sung, like 'interpretation', 'tempo', 'expression', 'pitch accuracy', 'rhythm', etc.

The study of music may include learning to listen and appreciate different kinds of music, as well as compose and perform one's own music. Some of the criteria under a heading like 'Composition' may show similarities with those in the preparing and production of works of art described above, as pupils seek inspiration, try out melodies and rhythms, select instruments or accompaniments, and create and improve their original musical piece.

Humanities

Subjects like geography, history and religious education, whether taught separately or in combination, involve an intricate mixture of factual knowledge, understanding of key concepts and principles, skills such as map reading, or tracing and analysing source documents, attitudes and values. This means that a wide and varied range of approaches to assessment may need to be employed.

Some aspects of assessment will be particularly sensitive. Religious beliefs, for example, are an especially personal matter, as are issues that regularly occur in humanities work, such as the role of the family in society, interpersonal relationships, ethical considerations, the rights and wrongs of historical or contemporary events. Many topics consist of a body of factual knowledge, which in itself may not be especially contentious, and a set of attitudes and values that go with them, which may. The facts about different sources of energy, for example, may be fairly clear, but arguments about the benefits they offer, or whether their effects on the environment outweigh their usefulness, may be more open to argument. The dates and details of historical events may be generally agreed, but interpretations and assessments of their impact or significance, of the moral rightness or wrongness of an individual or group, may be the subject of dispute.

One important issue in assessment of the humanities, therefore, is that while some attitudes and values may be difficult to appraise, when different but equally tenable views are well argued, all pupils' work should be well founded. A passionate but ill-informed treatise on 'pollution', or 'the use and misuse of power', should be assessed in such a way that the writer is encouraged to improve the work by substantiating what is being claimed with such evidence as is available. To do less is to perform a disservice to pupils, as they would not learn the value of evidence, nor the skills of seeking it out. The *resource-based essay* is a useful tool, both for learning and assessment. Children are provided with, and given the opportunity to find, a range of historical documents, geographical information or whatever, and can thus base their essay on sound data.

Language

Assessing pupils' native language and any foreign language that they may have learned can involve teachers in a variety of written and oral processes. Common components of such courses, whether taught separately or in an integrated way, include: learning to speak and listen to the language, to read and write it, and to become familiar with its literature and the culture of those who speak it. Each of these aspirations may be assessed separately or together. Oral competence, for example, can be appraised by asking pupils to speak about literature and culture, and writing skill can be assessed from pupils' written accounts of books they have read.

One issue which frequently occurs in the assessment of language is the extent to which inaccuracies in grammar, syntax, spelling or the spoken word should be corrected. It is sometimes assumed that linguistic accuracy and creativity must inevitably be in conflict. While it is probably true that to overwhelm a child with a welter of corrections and amendments, all at the same time, might be confusing, it is not true that attention to accuracy inhibits imagination. It is perfectly possible to aim at accurate use of language and also to value the imaginative use of it. In extreme forms, the one aim may interfere with the other, but many teachers are able to achieve speech and writing from pupils that are both correct and flowing, in their mother tongue or in a foreign language.

Oral assessment is especially time-consuming, as teachers usually need to hear pupils individually, and possibly keep a sound or video-taped record of key pieces of assessment. However, formative assessment is very important here, and it is possible to compile a series of consecutive tape recordings, over a period of time, both as records of achievement and as motivators for pupils who should be able to hear and monitor their own progress.

The teaching and assessment of reading, however, is the aspect of English, certainly in the early years, that usually attracts most public attention. This is hardly surprising, since parents and other citizens understandably see it as one of the most vital sets of skills that children need to acquire, if they are to cope successfully with our increasingly complex and fast-moving society. As a result of this high degree of interest both inside and outside schools, more time and effort has been put into designing and administering tests in reading than almost any other aspect of the curriculum.

Numerous forms of assessment are available in the field of reading. One problem is the sheer diversity of intent and focus in these many instruments. Some tests stress comprehension, so children are asked to read a passage and answer written or oral questions about it, or select an answer to a question from a set of alternatives. Others emphasise word recognition and sight vocabulary, so they often begin with simple two- and three-letter monosyllabic words and build up to more complex two-, three- and polysyllabic words.

One option is the 'cloze' test. This involves retyping a passage and missing out every seventh word or so, after a longer opening section has been reproduced to give a sense of meaning: 'Many people like to keep dogs as pets. If you own a dog, you can either let it sleep inside the house, or it can sleep outside in its kennel. A kennel is the name for a dog's ____. Some people don't particularly want their ____ to sleep outside when the weather ____ cold, so they let it sleep ____ the porch in winter.' Pupils have to fill in the missing words and teachers check how many acceptable words they can provide, like 'home' or 'house' in the case of the first gap. If they can provide two-thirds or more credible missing words, the assumption is that they can read that level of text independently, whereas 40% or less suggests the text may be too frustrating for them at this stage of their development.

Diagnostic tests and the analysis of pupils' reading errors, or 'miscues' as they are sometimes called, are also common. For example, if a pupil reads 'book' instead of 'boot', or 'trumpet' instead of 'trouble', this may suggest he is only looking at the initial letter and may need encouragement and support to scrutinise the whole of the word. Practice can then be given with words that have similar openings, but different endings, like 'can' and 'cat', 'fill' and 'fish', or 'sing' and 'silly'. Caution needs to be exercised, however, that words are learned in context, as well as out of it.

Mathematics

In theory mathematics is one of those subjects where the answers to problems are clearly right or wrong, so assessment appears straightforward, on the surface at least. With simple calculations this may be true, but even in these cases assessment will need to be more than mere correction of answers. If children are to make progress, then they must learn from their errors, and there is no guarantee that a tick or a cross will achieve this on its own. Unless they reflect on their workings, the model or analogue they used, and numerous other aspects of mathematical thinking, they may learn little.

As with many other subjects, pupils may not always do themselves justice if they lack language competence. Many mathematical problems are expressed in written prose: 'If x and y are the case … then calculate z'. Those with poor grasp of language may be unable to demonstrate their mathematical knowledge and skill. Language is an important part of learning in any subject.

One national test of mathematics for 7-year-olds illustrates this very well. At the simplest level children were given a set of coloured straws ranging in length from 9 cm to 20 cm. First they had to identify the longest and the shortest. Next they were asked to select three from the set to make the shortest possible line. They were then asked: 'How did you find the right straws for your line?' Marks were given for using words like short, shorter, shortest, not as long/short as … etc., but not for big, bigger, biggest, little, littler, littlest, on the grounds that these were not the most appropriate language of 'length'. Understanding a subject and its language may be inextricably linked.

The weighting of different aspects of mathematics assessment in public examinations may well have a considerable effect on the amount of time and energy devoted to it in school. Mathematics has a high profile in public debate, a matter that will be discussed again in Unit 6, and the equal weighting of several components may

Identifying the 'longest' and 'shortest' straws

produce a different response in schools compared with a policy of giving a high weighting to one or more particular aspects, like 'number' or 'measures'.

Science

In theory science involves much more precisely delineated concepts than many school subjects, so assessment ought to be more exact. In practice there are certainly many aspects of science where testing knowledge and understanding may appear straightforward, but there are still pitfalls for the unwary. Sometimes pupils may be able to give a mechanical response to a factual scientific question which is technically correct, yet not fully understand the principle, the relationship between cause and effect, the implications for other cases, the application of a law that has been learned, or the interpretation of results. For example, a student may be able to recite Boyle's law, stating quite correctly that 'the pressure and volume of gas are inversely proportional', without truly understanding what an 'inversely proportional' relationship actually means.

Since the learning of key concepts in science is so important, diagnostic testing can be very useful, especially over the matter of misconceptions. A simple way of attempting to assess what pupils may or may not understand is to offer a five-point scale on which they can reveal the confidence of their beliefs. They may be given statements about scientific principles, facts, laws or interpretations and asked to circle the appropriate response.

In a topic like 'Magnetism' they might be presented with a set of *misconceptions*, such as 'Magnets pick up objects with metal in them', 'The north poles of two magnets will stick together', mixed in with *correct assumptions*, like 'Magnets pick up objects with iron in them', or 'The north poles of two magnets will push each other away'. The five-point response scale might then be written as follows, with the answers circled, if they are not guesses, illustrating the degree of confidence students have in their understanding:

I know this is true
I think this is true
I am not sure
I think this is wrong
I know this is wrong

The responses would offer useful diagnostic information early in the study of the topic, or give a valuable insight into what had been learned after magnetism had been taught.

Vocational and practical courses

Teaching prevocational and vocational courses, as well as those with a strong practical element, like technology or physical education, can also bring into play a wide set of assessment procedures. Many of the points made about other subjects are applicable here too, but students' practical skills may have to be observed and evaluated *in situ*, in the workshop, in the gymnasium, swimming pool, or on the games field, in the office, or in a simulated work environment.

Courses of this kind require the assessor to be a shrewd observer of events and practices. It would be too easy to miss vital clues, so it is worth spending time reflecting on and planning the collection of evidence of competence. Several elements need to be prepared carefully, especially for formal assessments that are part of an award, including these:

- *The nature of the evidence* – what will be recorded and why?
- *The means by which it is collected* – will a written, sound or video record be made?
- *Ways of verifying what is observed* – will a

second evaluator check the findings?
- *The methods of grading or rating it* – how will competence be assessed?
- *The subsequent use of the evidence* – how will it be used and will there be feedback?

All these points are important. Once assessors have chosen to focus on one aspect rather than another, they have defined what is thought to be important. If evaluators of skill in a sport like football, for example, decided that ability to pass the ball to another player was particularly noteworthy, then they might easily miss other essential aspects of practical skill, such as scoring goals, tackling and winning the ball, or goalkeepers' saves.

The nature of the record kept is also vital. Human memory can be frail, even shortly after an event, so a written or taped record may be essential in many circumstances. Subjective judgement is inescapable in observation, so that is why verification is an issue, particularly during formal assessment for a qualification or award. A second observer may see things differently, or may confirm the judgement of the first observer. That is why the term 'consensus of those competent to judge' is sometimes used, as a single person's perceptions may be too partisan. Nowhere is this more apparent than in the assessment of teaching competence itself. Different observers sometimes have different perceptions of teaching skill, depending on their preferences and predispositions, and teachers often become upset if an observer is critical of their teaching.

Where two assessors disagree, the solution is not to 'split the difference'. All this does is push the marks towards the middle of the range. It also ignores the reason why two assessors differ so much. If one regards someone as a 'Grade B' and a second observer as a 'Grade D', then it would not be wise merely to settle on a 'Grade C'. There may be fundamental reasons why one mark is lower than the other. Perhaps one assessor has simply interpreted the marking conventions differently, or has been unduly impressed, or put off, by something that happened early in the assessment, when assessors can be most open to influence. 'Rate until agreement' is a better process. In other words, the two evaluators should discuss the reasons for their grading and negotiate an agreed grade, bringing in an arbitrator if they are deadlocked.

The nature of any ratings or gradings used is another crucial matter. *Rating scales* are often

Assessment 'in situ'

based on five or seven points, though some raters prefer an even-numbered scale with four or six points, to prevent assessors settling too easily for the 'neutral' middle grade. The evaluator simply circles one of the grades.

| Takes care | 1 2 3 4 5 6 7 | Is slipshod |
| Finishes work | 1 2 3 4 5 6 7 | Gives up easily |

There are problems with rating scales, including the tendency of evaluators to 'halo rate', that is, to make the preliminary general judgement of people as a 'Grade 2' or 'Grade 5' candidate, and therefore to give them very similar ratings on all the dimensions, reducing the reliability of the assessment, as was mentioned in Unit 2.

Another pitfall is 'recency', the tendency to be overly influenced by events that happen just before a final decision on the rating is made. If a pupil committed some slipshod act just as the observer was about to circle the number 3 on the scale above, then it might easily lead to the assessment becoming 5 or 6, despite previous events.

A third issue is the extent to which ratings can and should be applied to fields of knowledge and aspects of behaviour. This is especially relevant when complex behaviour is atomised into numerous tiny scales and checklists, as can happen in the assessment of vocational knowledge, skills and behaviour. The question must be asked whether the ability to perform dozens of discrete and separated acts can add up to an ability to do the job in a variety of circumstances.

To help overcome some of these problems, different kinds of rating scale have been developed. What are sometimes called, somewhat clumsily, *behaviourally anchored rating scales* (BARS) attempt to attach a description to each point, so that the assessor can see the type of performance that should be awarded that particular point. The five-point scale below shows an example of a range that covers various stages from ignorance of the basic principles to autonomy.

5 Understands fully the relevant principle and applies it without supervision in a variety of different situations.
4 Understands the relevant principle and applies it under supervision.
3 Understands the relevant principle, but cannot yet apply it in real-life situations.
2 Partially understands the relevant principle, but cannot apply it.
1 Does not understand the relevant principle and cannot apply it.

As is the case with other forms of assessment, the evaluation of practical and vocational competence often involves the compilation of headings and sub-headings under which judgements are made. These should reflect the nature of the activity under review and any weightings should be based on a rational appraisal of the relative importance of each aspect. Sometimes each of these is given a separate grade, as in the example below.

The strictures made above about the care that needs to be exercised so that complex behaviour is not merely reduced to a large cluster of separate micro-acts still applies, even when care has been taken to keep the overall concept and performance intact.

Feedback is particularly important in practical assessments. A crucial decision has to be made about the timing of it, and this may be affected by the nature of the activity. If someone's skill at a sport like tennis is being assessed and video recording is in use, then immediate feedback may be essential, so that pupils can see what their backhand looks like, act on advice to improve it, and then see once more, both during the action and also on video whether their strokes appear to be getting better. If the nature of feedback, however, is that someone needs to reflect first about their own performance, then a delay may be appropriate. Long delays, however, are rarely advisable, unless someone has developed a block to further learning and needs a break to enable a fresh start.

a ACTIVITY 9

Subject assessment

1 Choose a subject you are teaching to a particular class, selecting one element of it for careful analysis.
2 Devise a form of assessment of the pupils, ensuring that the assessment fits as closely as possible the demands of the particular subject, being clear in your mind of the purpose, what form it will take, how it will be assessed, how feedback will be given.
3 Make the assessment. Ask a fellow teacher or student teacher to assess the work independently using similar procedures.
4 Compare assessments, and discuss ways in which this form of assessment might be improved in future, concentrating on relating the assessment as closely as possible to the demands of the subject matter.

Summarise the observations made during the review period in the grid below. Tick *one* of the grades as follows: A = Excellent, outstanding performance; B = Good, more than meets the standard required for the award; C = Satisfactory, adequate for the award; D = Unsatisfactory, does not yet meet the standard for the award. Highest weighting should be given to items 1 and 2 when awarding the overall grade.

		A	B	C	D
1	Mastery of the relevant vocational knowledge	✓			
2	Mastery of the craft skills	✓			
3	Ability to work independently	✓			
4	Relationships with colleagues		✓		
5	Relationships with clients		✓		
6	Use of initiative	✓			
7	Ability to communicate in written form			✓	
8	Ability to communicate orally		✓		
OVERALL ASSESSMENT		✓			

5 If possible and desirable, discuss the assessment with some of the pupils, asking them what they think they have learned about the subject matter through the kind of assessment you have used.

6 Try out a similar task with a similar group of pupils on a later occasion, incorporating what you have learned.

SELF-ASSESSMENT

Learning to assess one's own work is fraught with difficulties, but that is not necessarily a reason for avoiding self-assessment. 'Self-confrontation', as it is sometimes called, may have a varying impact on learners. For some it can be highly illuminating, making them party to their own learning, offering a sense of ownership. They can feel that they are in the driving seat, acquiring the sort of autonomy that mature adults achieve when they are able to review what they are doing and make their own judgements about how to improve it. For others it may be debilitating, imparting a sense of failure by inviting them to strip off their defences, many of which may have become well oiled. Some people can be very hard on themselves, destroying their self-confidence in the process. Self-evaluation, if it is to exert a positive effect on learning, needs to be introduced, carried out and monitored in a sensitive and thoughtful manner.

There are many forms of self-assessment, and they may need to be varied to suit the ages and background of the pupils. With younger children, for example, not yet able to write in depth about their work, it may be possible to use, as a form of shorthand, a series of iconic 'smiley' faces, showing varying degrees of satisfaction or dissatisfaction with what they have done.

I have done this well ☺
This is OK (about my usual standard)
I have not done this as well as I can ☹

The same kind of icons can be used to assess behaviour in class, attitudes to topics or issues ('I agree/disagree with …', 'I like/do not like …'), effort ('I have/have not been trying hard …'), or general progress in a particular field of study.

Structure

While it may be possible for pupils to assess their own work according to their own criteria, it may also be necessary to give them some clues about the form this might take. Just as teachers and external examiners often need an agreed marking scheme of some kind, so too may pupils. Indeed, working out criteria for assessment, what should be weighted, what constitutes 'good', 'accurate', 'imaginative', 'successful' work, whether literal grades (A, B, C, etc.), numerical marks, or written comments will be necessary, can itself be very insightful for pupils, allowing them to discuss and argue about the purpose of the exercise and what is valued. In the case of public examinations, it can be even more illuminating for them to apply the 'official' marking scheme to their own attempts at answering questions.

Checklists

In order to help pupils look for important elements in their work, teachers can sometimes offer a checklist. This is particularly useful in areas where the essential features, concepts, or elements are clearly known in advance. For example, if a pupil is asked to draw an insect, the checklist might read:

1 Have you drawn and labelled the three parts of the body – head, abdomen and thorax?
2 Have you drawn two or four wings?
3 Has the insect got the right number of legs (six)?
4 Have you drawn the antennae?

Checklists often consist of yes/no answers or boxes to tick, but it is important not to take their use too far. Some areas simply do not have clear-cut 'right answers'. The answer to a subtraction sum may be unambiguous, but the merits or otherwise of a poem are more open to argument.

Self-assessment checklists should not suffocate pupils by merely reifying the teacher's own opinions, stifling legitimate dissent, or ruling out valid alternative solutions where these exist. Their major use is to stimulate active learning. If pupils have to think about their answers and the rest of their work, rather than simply hand them in for someone else to reflect on, then this may help them learn more effectively. They are enabled to evaluate what they have learned, and are also given the opportunity to rectify any omissions or misconceptions by their own hand.

Self-correction

This is not quite the same as a checklist, which offers pointers for reflection. 'Self-correction' here is taken to mean that the pupil is given an answer sheet, a set of 'correct' responses. This can only work when there is no ambiguity and little or no choice. In the case of mathematics, for example, pupils can be given the answers to the maths problems they have to solve. The major use, therefore, is in the area of information recall, and also problem solving where there is a single correct answer: 'What is the capital of France?', 'When was the Battle of Hastings?', 'What is the German word for "child"?', 'Who painted the Mona Lisa?', 'What is 498 + 375?'.

Self-correction can also be used where there is more than one acceptable response, but only if these are limited, rather than open-ended. The answer to the test item 'Name two inert gases' must come from the list 'argon, helium, krypton, neon, radon and xenon', since there are only six of them. An item like 'Name two great painters', on the other hand, would be far too problematic and diffused for simple self-correction. It would be difficult to define the word 'great' with sufficient precision and, second, to list the huge number of painters over the centuries who might arguably qualify for this accolade.

Some tests, particularly those with 'closed' answers, like 'True/False', or multiple-choice papers where only one response is correct, are sometimes referred to as *self-marking*. This means that a card with holes in can be put over the answer paper, like a template, so that the pupil can see at a glance which answers are correct, as these are the ones whose boxes will show up through the holes. Many tests nowadays are machine-scored in this way, and the machine simply reads the number of shaded boxes or ticks that are in the right spaces. Handy though this may be for assessors faced with thousands of multiple-choice scripts, they are of limited value for pupils, unless someone takes the time to discuss incorrect answers with them. They may enable pupils to calculate their total score, but they do not always, on their own, illuminate and analyse incorrect reasoning, inadequate factual knowledge, or the nature of misconceptions.

Peer assessment

Closely related to self-assessment is peer assessment. This involves fellow pupils assessing each other's work. A pair of children, for example, may exchange test papers or assignments and each evaluate the quality, accuracy, appropriateness of what the other has done. Many of the same points made above are relevant here. Pupils will usually need some structure and support if they are to assess fairly and informatively. There is no point in compounding errors and misconceptions by having one ill-informed child pass on incorrect judgements to another.

Peer assessment also needs to be carefully prepared. It cannot be assumed that every pupil automatically knows how to make an appropriate and factually correct response in all circumstances. The context is also important. If children are working in competition with each other, they may be harsh or even unfair in their appraisal of what they see as their 'competitors'. Even if they are meant to work collaboratively, they may not always behave harmoniously.

Dr Martin Underwood of Exeter University has developed a programme in physical education (Underwood, 1991) in which pupils have to assess one another as they work together to improve their gymnastic skill. In the research and development work that preceded the publication of the course, three boys were observed working together, one holding a work card on which a set of movements was illustrated. Their task was to help each other improve their own performance of each movement. Two pupils tried to work out a paired movement, as shown in the pictures they had, while the third helped them do it better. They then swapped roles, so that each had a chance both to perform with a partner and to appraise the others.

When the third boy, Ian, took his turn as coach to the other two pupils, he derided their performance. 'You're clueless, Gareth,' Ian laughed. 'You've no idea. You're a complete Digby' ('Digby' is the name of the local mental hospital, used as a term of abuse). The class's teacher came over and explained patiently that the whole idea was that they should help each other improve, not just show contempt. 'See what you think is going wrong and try to come up with something constructive,' he said to Ian. 'Gareth didn't laugh at you when you were doing it.'

The two boys carried on, and Ian suggested that if Gareth straightened his back, then the

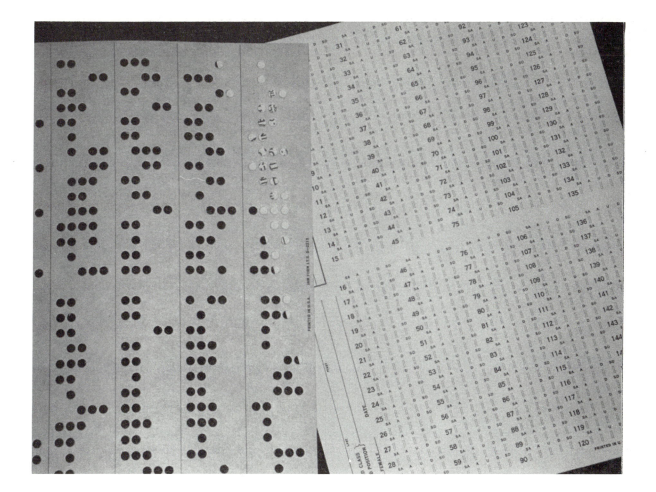

Self-scoring test (*right*) and marking template (*left*)

movement might work better. Teacher monitoring and intervention when necessary is essential if peer assessment is to work positively. In the case just described, the pupils were able to learn something valuable not just in the field of gymnastics but also in terms of their own personal and social development.

Personal and social development and behaviour

Personal, social and moral education are cross-disciplinary fields, like 'citizenship', 'health education', 'the environment', 'thinking', which can loop across several subjects, or be taught in their own right as subjects on the timetable. I have written about this view of the curriculum elsewhere (Wragg, 1997). If assessment is to be closely reflective of, and therefore linked to, the curriculum itself, then pupil learning and development may well be evaluated using many of the means described elsewhere in this book.

Personal attributes, learning and behaviour are extraordinarily sensitive matters. Young children have to learn to be members not only of their school class or peer group, but also of their family and community in the wider society in which they live, now and in the future. On the one hand, therefore, they need to conform to many of the norms and conventions inside and outside school, the rules and laws that govern society and which citizens need to observe if they are to fulfil their obligations to their fellows. They also need to develop as individuals, able to act autonomously, rather than have to wait to be told what to do next.

There can sometimes be some tension between the development and the evaluation of the individual, and that person's role in the group. Many great inventions are the result of people being willing to break with convention and try an unorthodox solution. Flight is one example. Early attempts to develop flying machines were trapped into the model of birds with flapping wings, so they were too cumbersome and unwieldy to take off. The solution of trying rigid wings seemed illogical. How could something fly if its wings did not move? Yet the unconventional approach was the one that worked.

The assessment of personal, social and moral education needs to be handled with consummate skill. There has to be a balance between personal and social development. It is not impossible to sponsor both. Indeed, part of learning in both areas is reconciling the sometimes conflicting demands of individual and group needs. Informal and formative assessment are likely to be much more common than formal and summative assessment. Many adults will testify to the positive effects teachers had on their development in these areas by sensitive feedback during crucial years of their development, just as others will bear deep scars from insensitive assessment of their person when their self-esteem or confidence was low. This is not an argument against assessment in these sensitive areas of human development, rather one for its being carried out skilfully.

WHOLE SCHOOL ISSUES

The points that were made in Unit 5 about personal and social development have some relevance to the role of teachers in a school. Teachers are individual professionals, able to make certain choices about how they assess their class in its various subjects and activities, but they are also members of a team. Having a 'whole school' policy towards assessment, and how it might foster learning, need not rob teachers of all their autonomy. Such a policy does not mean that every teacher must assess in an identical manner, whether teaching younger or older pupils, mathematics or history, examination or non-examination classes. It simply means that any group of teachers needs to know what common themes and practices have been endorsed, and what kind of differences exist.

The process of discussion and negotiation can help teachers in a school develop their own ideas on assessment. It is perfectly possible, for example, that a school might develop its own form of student profile, which records pupils' progress and experiences throughout their school career. However, such a profile, though in common use, would need to recognise the different styles of assessment that may be applied in different subjects and activities, or as children move higher up the school. A record of a maths test devised and given by a teacher at the end of a year does not have to look exactly the same as pupils' personal written records of what they did and what they learned on a geography field trip.

Several issues are worth discussing when schools draw up an assessment policy. They include the following:

- *Planning* What kinds of informal and formal assessment by teachers and pupils will be used in different contexts and who will be responsible for them.
- *Learning* The positive steps that will be taken to ensure that children learn something from being assessed, so that teachers and pupils can see clearly the place of assessment in teaching and learning.
- *Marking* What the major conventions on marking are likely to be, and whether, for example, there will be a 'guarantee' that work handed in will normally be marked and returned within a stated time.
- *Recording* How progress will be recorded, what individual teacher records and cumulative records will be kept in the school, who will have access to these.
- *Reporting* Communication within the school about assessment, and also communication with those outside the school, like parents and others who have a right to know.

In this unit we shall consider classroom matters that are worth discussing and developing across the school, like marking, profiling, recording and reporting, as well as wider matters such as staff development and teacher appraisal, the inspection of schools, and the public display of assessment information in league tables.

MARKING

The original Old High German word *marcon*, from which 'marking' is derived, meant 'setting out a boundary'. This involved drawing a line on the ground, or putting down stones or other indicators to show where one territory ended and another began. The term now has much broader meaning, but in assessment that uses grading, or categorises work in some way, the original definition persists. Indeed, public examination boards have to spend a great deal of their effort on determining the boundaries between one grade and the next, as thousands of candidates often fall on the borderline.

As has been described in previous units, the actual marking of pupils' work will be influenced by the particular nature of the subject, topic, or activity, and the philosophy of those who teach it. Whether they use impressionistic marking, or systematically draw up a scoring grid that assigns so many marks to each section or element of the assessment, is often an individual matter. However, sharing intentions, experiences and conventions is something that can be done as part of natural staff discussion about issues of mutual concern when planning, analysing, or changing policy and practice.

In daily classroom life, there are several aspects of marking that are worthy of reflection and debate. They include the ones below.

Correction

What, if any, marks, comments, corrections should teachers put on children's work? Consider the following three examples, written by pupils.

Example A	'Insects have eight legs.'
Example B	'They loked for accomodation in a cheep hotel.'
Example C	'Ravel's *Bolero* is undoubtedly the finest piece of music ever written.'

Example A is simply wrong. Insects have six legs, so the teacher has to make a choice. She could write alongside the statement 'Wrong! They have six legs.' She might underline the word 'eight' and write 'NO' over the top of it. Or she may decide to make the pupil think by simply putting a question mark above the word 'eight' and writing 'Are you sure?'. She may write nothing on the pupil's book, but discuss it with her instead. There are other possibilities, including ignoring the error and doing nothing, which would be inadvisable in my view.

Example B is a correct statement, but it contains three spelling errors, 'loked', 'accomodation' and 'cheep'. Again the teacher has choices which include: writing correct spellings above each error, using some kind of shorthand to indicate a spelling error, such as 'S' or 'Sp', but not actually giving the child the correct version, and so on.

Example C may well be a correct statement as far as the individual child is concerned, since she is especially enthusiastic about Ravel's piece, but her assertion that it is 'undoubtedly' the finest work of music ever composed is manifestly wrong. It is an example of a pupil writing an unsubstantiated generalisation. Once more the teacher has choices. She may write in the margin 'No, it isn't' (an equally unsubstantiated statement!), 'Who says?', or 'That may be your opinion, but it is not necessarily the view of others'. She may indicate the type of error she thinks has been committed by underlining the word 'undoubtedly' and writing 'What is your evidence for saying this?'.

Several factors may influence what action is taken to correct work. I have never personally believed, for example, that to write on a pupil's book is likely to destroy the child's confidence. It depends entirely on what is written and what messages go with it. The statement 'This is appalling' is totally different from 'Satisfactory', or 'This is an excellent story, very well written. Make sure you use the apostrophe properly'. There is a problem when children make several errors and correcting every single one at the same time could be overwhelming, but this is not an argument for taking no action, rather one for picking out some of the areas that need special help.

If children are to learn from their assessment, then correction of errors and discussion of what they have done is essential. Questions to be faced over marking include: whether to give correct forms or make pupils think about them for themselves; what kind of signs or comments to write on work, and whether to indicate these at the appropriate place in the pupil's book or at the end; what to do with children who make numerous errors or appear generally bewildered by the task; how to follow up the assessment to encourage children to learn from their mistakes and build on what they know, rather than get demoralised.

Recording

Which elements of the mass of formal and informal assessments that are made over a school career should be recorded in some semi-permanent or permanent form? If there were no records, then it would be difficult to see what progress had been made. On the other hand, if too much time is spent on recording, then valuable energy may be sucked away from teaching and learning. Judicious choices have to be made about what is worth preserving.

Not only must decisions be made about what should be recorded, but agreement needs to be reached about the form of records, especially if assessment is seen to be a continuous and formative process, rather then a series of disconnected rituals. The following all constitute records of one kind or another, but they are expressed in quite different forms.

- Grade B
- Level 4
- 61%
- Satisfactory work and progress.
- Above average in algebra and probability, average in number and measures.
- Has read several new books, including one by Roald Dahl, but still lacks decoding skills with new words, tending to guess from initial letters.

Some are norm-referenced, though unspecific, only meaningful if one knows the context fully. The last of the comments above is more diagnostic than the others. A record that states 'Level 4' can only mean something if the criteria for achieving Level 4 are available for reference. A score like 61%, especially if transmitted to parents, may also mean little. A pupil may score 61%, yet have the lowest mark in his class in that particular subject. In a different subject, in the same class, 61% may be the highest mark.

If norm-referenced numerical scores are used across several subjects, then it is worth discussing whether these should be converted to *standard scores*. There are many ways of standardising scores and grades, usually described in detail in books that give the mathematical formulae for such calculations (e.g. Satterly, 1981; Frith and Macintosh, 1984). One common procedure is to convert the marks to what are called *T scores*. This means they come out with an average of 50 and a *standard deviation* of 10. Readers not familiar with the measure of distribution known as the 'standard deviation' will find it explained in most elementary statistics books.

In practice, conversion to T scores means that about two-thirds of the class will score 10 points either side of the mean, that is, between 40 and 60. The conversion to standard scores is quite simple to work out and there are computer programs available for doing it quickly. However, those wanting to use standard scores in their reporting should make sure they go through a worked example and understand the limits of what they are doing.

Reporting

Assessment is no longer a private and confidential matter. Pressures for public accountability require teachers to communicate some of their assessments to others. This may involve a national agency, if there is a teacher assessment of pupils' progress, or if coursework forms part of the examination. The school's procedures have to be impeccable, as external awards are usually open to close scrutiny. This can bring external moderators on a visit to the school to see how pupils' work is set, collected, marked and graded, as well as to vet security and record-keeping procedures. Any slackness in the arrangements is likely to lead to severe criticism.

National examining bodies are not the only external group that may be sent reports on pupils' achievements. Quite rightly, parents are also entitled to be told the results of certain key assessments when they become known. They must also be sent school reports showing their children's progress. One important focus in discussions about school policy is on procedures for reporting to parents. What information should be sent home, and when? Is it in user-friendly form, so that it will mean something to parents?

How are parents' evenings and meetings being used? Are the discussions jargon-free? It is easy for teachers to use technical terms about *levels*, *competencies*, *percentiles*, or *examination grades* without realising that the parent who appears to be nodding at the remarks does not fully understand what they mean. Without patronising parents, it is not too difficult to find a diplomatic way of explaining any essential terms: 'I don't know whether you're familiar with the latest version of the curriculum, but "Level 4" in mathematics means that he can do things like ...', or 'Since Jane is hoping to go on to university, it's important that she tries to make sure she gets at least grade ...'. Teachers of the more complex vocational courses can even find themselves saying, in all honesty: 'These assessment procedures are so complicated, I have to keep explaining them to parents so I understand them myself!'

Parents

The question is sometimes asked whether there is a place for parents in the assessment of their own children's work. It is a delicate matter for several reasons:

1 Some parents are highly educated, while others are not, so there will be considerable differences in their understanding of the subject matter.
2 Some parents may seek to favour their own child by offering generous assessments, or genuinely find it difficult to see their own children's mistakes and correct them.
3 Other parents may be overly severe and have little understanding of what pupils of a certain age can do, or may have exaggerated their own prowess as children.
4 Putting parents in the role of 'assessor' may affect family relationships.

What role can parents play in assessment?

Norm-referenced assessment, therefore, is difficult, because most parents cannot know what sort of range of performance children of a certain age are achieving. Nonetheless, there are some assessing and auditing functions that can be considered. They include such possibilities as: parents checking whether their children's homework has been done, or whether they have read the book they have taken home, and perhaps countersigning a record of it; helping their children carry out a 'self-marking' exercise, as described earlier, when the answers are provided and children can check whether their responses are correct or not; confirming that pupils have actually done what they claim to have done outside school hours in their 'record of achievement'.

Profiling

The use of pupil profiles is a school-wide issue, because different teachers may be contributing to it as a child's career progresses. There are numerous forms of pupil profile and most contain a mixture of records of grades or levels of attainment in various subjects, as well as indicators of personal qualities, hobbies and interests, achievements in fields not on the timetable, and other data. Many are simple, some are elaborate.

One matter worth considering is that of audience. For which individuals or groups are the profiles being compiled? For future employers? Teachers? Parents? The pupils themselves? Or all

of these? The nature of the audience to some extent determines the form and style of a profile. If pupils are to learn from their profile, then they should be fully engaged in compiling the record. A profile can be seen as a personal record of experience and achievement for pupils, rather than merely as something done to them.

There are many possible components, so the first-order questions must be about the purposes and principles of having a profiling system in place. Only when these are clear can the detailed content be worked out. If the profile is to offer formative, not just summative records, then it must be in such a form that it can be completed along the way, rather than filled in solely at the end of a year or phase. A formative record is in any case more likely to be influential on children's learning. Whether the profile is diagnostic, the extent to which academic, pastoral and external elements feature, the elements completed by the teacher or supervisor and those entered by pupils themselves, the extent to which group and team work as well as individual work should be incorporated, who may see the profile and who eventually 'owns' it, all these are matters deserving careful scrutiny.

While profiles for younger pupils may be chiefly aimed at providing them, their teachers and their parents with a cumulative record of their primary schooling, for older pupils the profile often represents a document that may be shown to an employer. There have been numerous surveys of employers' concerns about new employees, and many of them have to do with personal qualities like attendance, punctuality, effort, reliability, willingness to co-operate, application, working with others, responsibility, initiative, leadership and confidence (Broadfoot, 1987). Some of these are easier areas to assess than others. 'Punctuality' may simply be a record of how many times a pupil has arrived late, while 'confidence' is an aspect of personality that can easily deceive. People may appear confident on the surface, but resemble a jelly inside.

Some elements of a profile aimed at employers may mimic the 'competency' approach inherent in many vocational qualifications and offer a 'can do' format, like 'Can work independently', 'Can dismantle and reassemble a carburettor', or 'Can plot graphs and histograms accurately, labelling axes and units correctly'. These may be useful, but if they become too numerous and detailed, then it is difficult for the reader to find the whole person amidst the mass of atomic particles.

At their best, profiles can offer a comprehensive record of what pupils have done over a period of several years, giving them and others a much fuller picture than could be obtained from a set of grades alone. They can also be influential on pupils' learning, especially if they contain a mixture of contributions from teachers, pupils themselves and other appropriate sources.

If not handled skilfully, however, they can become bureaucratic, cumbersome and time-consuming, and they can also stigmatise and stereotype pupils if they are unable to shake off earlier assessments, especially when these are negative and bruising. This last point raises the important matter of the place of negative and positive appraisals. Some teachers believe that profiles should be entirely positive, showing only what pupils can do, rather than highlighting what they cannot achieve, or their negative characteristics. The contrary argument, however, is that completely positive profiles may not portray pupils as they really are, giving a false picture to the reader. This is a debate that should not be confined to teachers, as pupils could profitably join in it as part of their personal development.

Assessment bias and equal opportunities

Even though many schools make every effort to ensure that their assessment procedures are fair, there are numerous pitfalls for the unwary. These include test bias, stereotyped or overly subjective evaluations, and lack of opportunity to learn or take part in the assessment.

Test bias of various kinds can be present even in the most carefully conceived forms of assessment. Gipps (1990) gives several examples of how one language test may show superiority for boys rather than girls, while another, with a different focus, perhaps based on comprehension rather than vocabulary, may show the opposite result. Children from different ethnic and social groups may be disadvantaged in certain tests or individual items not because their competence is lower, but because of cultural differences.

Gipps quotes an interesting example from an analysis of reading test responses by Hannon and McNally (1986) in which the following sentence insertion item was used:

Jimmy _____ tea, because he was our guest.

   1) washed the dishes after
   2) was late for
   3) got the best cake at
   4) could not eat his

The 'correct' answer was supposed to be number (3), and most middle-class children gave this response. Some 60% of working-class and bilingual children chose number (1). In some cultures, it would be appropriate to wash up out of gratitude for the invitation. For certain children the test may, therefore, be an indicator of social behaviour, rather than an accurate measure of reading ability.

a ACTIVITY 10

Equal opportunities?

There are many questions that can be asked, when schools review the matter of possible bias or unequal opportunities. Analyse your own lessons and those of other teachers: talk to them and observe their lessons and assessment practices, if possible, with the following agenda:

1 *Do all children have the opportunity to learn?*
   (a) Do some children get more of the teacher's time?
   (b) Do certain pupils regularly seize the equipment or the computer at the expense of others?

(c) Does the teacher address questions more to certain individuals or groups and ignore others?

2 *Are there any biases in the forms of assessment that are used that could be remedied or reduced?*
   (a) Are any of the tests used unfairly loaded against any individuals or groups?
   (b) Although different pupils may have different levels of resource at home, is there anything the school can do through its school or local library or resource centre?

3 *If certain individuals or groups do appear to have fewer or less satisfactory opportunities, who are they?*
   (a) Which individuals or groups seem to miss out or have a bad deal?
   (b) What can be done to enhance their opportunities or reduce the odds against them?

EXTERNAL INSPECTION AND PUBLIC INFORMATION

It is a central feature of public accountability nowadays that a school's assessment procedures and the results of the assessment of pupil learning are made publicly available, as was described above. In addition to the reports that may be sent to examination boards or parents, schools are open to external inspection and their results will be published in their prospectuses and in such league tables as may be drawn up and given to the press and broadcasting media. In recent years both inspections and league tables have generated considerable interest, and in some cases near hysteria, in the mass media.

School inspection

When inspectors visit a school, assessment procedures often come under close scrutiny in one form or another. First of all, inspection is bound to focus on the school's policy and practice, the extent to which informal and formal assessment are used effectively. The official framework to which inspectors have to work usually mentions this aspect of school life specifically. It is not something that will be left to the individual whim of inspectors. This means that schools will have to explain and justify how

they assess pupils' work, keep records and report to external bodies and to parents.

Second, the results of the school's public examinations and national tests are part of what is sometimes called the 'evidence base' on which inspectors may draw when making judgements about the school and the teaching and learning that take place within it. It is not unreasonable that such information should be scrutinised, but often the data are used crudely. Norm-referenced statements like 'The results in mathematics are well below/well above the national average' *on their own* say little about the quality of teaching and learning in the school, as they do not take into account the many different starting points. Some schools with children of high ability may have too low expectations, but still show above average performance on tests because of the efforts of parents or private tuition. Obversely, schools with large numbers of children with significant learning difficulties may struggle to obtain a set of grades close to the national average.

In combination with other evidence, however, test scores and teacher assessments may be of much greater interest, especially if inspectors use their knowledge of a wide range of schools to compare a school with others operating in similar circumstances. External inspection can be traumatic for teachers and heads, as their very persons seem to be under scrutiny, not just their professional practice. It is easy to become defensive and feel grateful when an inspection is over, especially if it appears mechanical and remote in form, emphasising paperwork and administrative procedures, rather than good practice in the classroom. Tempting though this may be, it might anaesthetise people to what needs to be done, so it is better to keep an open mind about the effectiveness of a school's assessment procedures and the actual results of pupil assessment. Good inspectors and advisers can offer valuable insights into what can be achieved, even in adverse circumstances, though it is a pity that not all inspection frameworks permit such advice and comparative insights to be given.

League tables

There is something seductive about league tables. They appear on the surface to be rich in precision. Average scores for each school can be cited to two decimal places. The public is used to seeing league tables in sporting events, when at the end of each season the champions are crowned and feted, and the losers are relegated. League tables look neat and precise, even if they have been built on sand.

Unfortunately, when league tables of pupil assessments are assembled, they are much more frail than they seem. Schools high in the tables, for reasons mentioned above, may not be those where the teaching and learning is of the best quality, especially when the league tables report raw scores.

There are, of course, procedures for adjusting raw scores. Statistical techniques, like *multiple regression* and *analysis of covariance*, can be used to take background factors into account. In simple terms, the process involves finding measures that correlate highly with pupil achievement, like 'intelligence', 'prior knowledge', or 'social background'. These are then used to rub out those parts of achievement scores that appear to be influenced by such factors, rather than by the quality of teaching and learning in the school.

To take a simplified example: two pupils, Janet and John, obtain 40% and 60% respectively on a test. On the surface it looks as if John must have worked harder and been taught better, as he has scored 20% more than Janet. But suppose that Janet spoke no English at the beginning of the school year, has no books in the home, no help from parents, and has worked enormously hard against the odds with a lot of skilful help from a dedicated teacher. In these circumstances 40% may be a remarkable achievement. Suppose, by contrast, John obtained 80% on a similar test last year, has made little effort this year, has been taught by a teacher who did not bother much whether he worked or not, and lives in a home with plenty of books. In this case 60% is not so impressive. League tables of raw scores, therefore, do not tell the whole story.

But supposing we adjusted Janet's and John's scores. Let us suppose that we use one of the approved statistical techniques to partial out the effects of John's privilege and prior achievement and Janet's lack of them. This might result in so much of each score being rubbed out that relatively little is left. So what would it mean to interpret differences in just the few percentage points that remain? Adjusted league tables are not necessarily all that more illuminating or 'fair' than unadjusted ones.

Another issue for a school in the context of league tables is the effect they may have on policy and practice. In the case of public examinations, for example, if the criterion on which they are based is *average number of 'passes' per pupil*, then

the pressure is to enter able pupils for far more subjects than is necessary to push up the batting average. If *percentage of 'passes' out of total entries* is the criterion, then the school may be reluctant to enter borderline candidates in case they fail. Even the fair-looking criterion *average grade per pupil*, counting all pupils on roll, may affect policy and practice. Schools may seek to disapply the national curriculum for pupils with special needs, so they are not assessed, or they may become reluctant to admit any children with learning difficulties, in case they let the side down.

The nearest league tables might come to reflecting true 'value added' would be if valid and reliable *baseline assessment* were available on entry. In other words, if there were some accurate measure of performance on entry against which future assessments might be compared. One difficulty is that baseline measures for 5-year-olds starting school tend to be fairly simple teacher assessments of language, number, personality or aptitude, so they are not always closely related to the many specific academic subjects that might be assessed a few years later. Once pupils are embarked on their education, however, baseline assessment on entry to junior or secondary school may be more varied and more closely related to subsequent school learning. Even so, 'value added' league tables, like other forms, still need to be used with some caution.

The problem is once more that of trying to make one single form of assessment serve too many purposes. One informal diagnostic test of reading is to say to a pupil, 'Read me an extract from your current book.' A number of aspects of reading competence would soon become reasonably clear, such as whether the child was coping or struggling, what kind of errors were being made, whether the pupil appeared to understand the text and could talk about it or was reading mechanically and without comprehension. However, this approach would be useless as a measure of standards over time or between groups without a great deal of additional analysis. One child might be reading from *War and Peace* and another from a book of nursery rhymes.

Equally, a standardised test, which measured adequately the ability of children to recognise simple and complex words, would be limited as a diagnostic test if it merely offered a standardised score but nothing else on which to build a future programme of reading. There is no single assessment tool that can compare standards between groups or over time, diagnose difficulties, inform pupils and parents in a meaningful way of progress, and be perfectly suited to each individual as well as to a whole group. That is why a variety of approaches is essential and why the strengths and limitations of any one form of assessment need to be borne in mind when interpreting results.

Staff development

Many of the points that have been covered in this book can be included in a programme of staff development. However, in the Leverhulme study of teacher appraisal which I directed (Wragg *et al.*, 1996) assessment was not high on teachers' lists of targets to be addressed during their appraisal. Only 4% of teachers in a national sample of over 1,100 included it as one of their priorities.

I have written more fully elsewhere (Wragg, 1994) about staff development and the role of the 'dynamic teacher' in the 'dynamic school', that is, the person who is not only able to reflect on current practice, but is also capable of making judicious changes along with others. This can create a climate in which a school constantly seeks to improve what it does and is thus dynamic rather than static. Staff development can offer opportunities for both individual and collaborative analysis and for subsequent action

on the central purposes and processes in the school. Assessment can be one of the areas considered.

There have been many suggestions throughout this book about activities that can help focus attention on different aspects of assessment. Assessment, like teaching itself, consists of thousands of repeats and rehearsals of sometimes similar, sometimes different actions. During their career, teachers lay down deep structures which inform their actions. Careful reflection followed by deliberate efforts to change practice for the better are essential if they are to improve their professional skill. There are many constraints of time and energy, but staff development activities can focus on a variety of topics.

Assessment is at least as important as many of the other features of in-service programmes, and much more important than some, not just to teachers but to the pupils, whose learning can be positively enhanced when assessment is handled with care and skill. This last point is a most important one. Throughout any staff development work the question constantly needs to be asked: 'How will any changes we make to our policies and practice actually improve pupils' learning?' If assessment and learning are ever divorced, then the former will become a barren bureaucratic exercise and the latter will be much the poorer for its detachment.

REFERENCES

Ashworth, A.E. (1982) *Testing for Continuous Assessment*, London: Evans Brothers.

Becker, W.C. and Engelmann, S. (1976) *Teaching 3: Evaluation of Instruction*, Chicago: Science Research Associates.

Beggs, D.L. and Lewis, E.L. (1975) *Measurement and Evaluation in the Schools*, Boston: Houghton Mifflin.

Boyle, B. and Christie, T. (eds) (1996) *Issues in Setting Standards: Establishing Comparabilities*, London: The Falmer Press.

Broadfoot, P. (1987) *Introducing Profiling: A Practical Manual*, Basingstoke: Macmillan.

Brown, G.A. and Wragg, E.C. (1993) *Questioning*, London: Routledge.

Burghes, D. and Blum, W. (1995) 'The Exeter–Kassel Comparative Project' in Gatsby Charitable Foundation, *Proceedings of a Seminar on Mathematics Education*, London, February 1995, 13–28.

Child, D. (1977) *Psychology and the Teacher*, London: Holt, Rinehart & Winston.

Davie, R., Butler, N. and Goldstein, H. (1972) *From Birth to Seven*, London: Longman.

Desforges, C. (1989) *Testing and Assessment*, London: Cassell.

Ebel, R.L. (1965) *Measuring Educational Achievement*, Englewood Cliffs: Prentice-Hall.

Foxman, D., Ruddock, G. and McCallum, I. (1990) *APU Mathematics Modelling 1984/88 (Phase 2)*, London: SEAC.

Frith, D.S. and Macintosh, H.G. (1984) *A Teacher's Guide to Assessment*, Cheltenham: Stanley Thornes.

Gipps, C. (1990) *Assessment: A Teacher's Guide to the Issues*, London: Hodder & Stoughton.

Goldstein, H. and Lewis, T. (eds) (1996) *Assessment: Problems, Development and Statistical Issues*, Chichester: John Wiley.

Green, J.A. (1963) *Teacher-Made Tests*, New York: Harper & Row.

Gronlund, N.E. (1985) *Measurement and Evaluation in Teaching*, New York: Macmillan.

Hannon, P. and McNally, J. (1986) 'Children's Understanding and Cultural Factors in Reading Test Performance', *Educational Review*, 38, 3, 237–246.

Harris, D. and Bell, C. (1990) *Evaluating and Assessing for Learning*, London: Kogan Page.

Kounin, J.S. (1970) *Discipline and Group Management in Classrooms*, New York: Holt, Rinehart & Winston.

Levy, P. and Goldstein, H. (1984) *Tests in Education: A Book of Critical Reviews*, London: Academic Press.

McLean, L.D. (1996) 'Large-Scale Assessment Programmes in Different Countries and International Comparisons', in Goldstein, H. and Lewis, T. (eds) *Assessment: Problems, Development and Statistical Issues*, Chichester: John Wiley.

Plowden Report (1967) *Children and Their Primary Schools*, Report of the Central Advisory Council for Education, London: HMSO.

Postlethwaite, T.N. (1987) *Comparative Education Review*, Special Issue, 31, 1.

Satterly, D. (1981) *Assessment in Schools*, Oxford: Basil Blackwell.

Underwood, A.M. (1991) *Agile*, Walton on Thames: Thomas Nelson.

Wragg, E.C. (1993) *Primary Classroom Skills*, London: Routledge.

Wragg, E.C. (1994) *An Introduction to Classroom Observation,* London: Routledge.

Wragg, E.C. (1997) *The Cubic Curriculum,* London: Routledge.

Wragg, E.C., Wikeley, F.J., Wragg, C.M. and

Haynes, G.S. (1996) *Teacher Appraisal Observed,* London: Routledge.

Young, M. and McGeeney, P. (1968) *Learning Begins at Home,* London: Routledge & Kegan Paul.